I0067205

DOS, DON'TS & PROFIT

How to **Prepare** Yourself and **Find** the Right Business to Buy

You Can't
Buy It
If You Can't
Find It

Ted J. Leverette

BUSINESS BUYER ADVOCATE®

How to Prepare Yourself and Find the Right Business to Buy
Copyright 2018-2021 Ted J. Leverette

Published by Partner On-Call Network, LLC
North Palm Beach, FL
PartnerOnCall.com

All rights reserved. No part of this publication may be reproduced, stored in or introduced into a public retrieval system or transmitted in any form or by any means (electronic, mechanical, photocopying, recording or otherwise) without the prior written permission of Ted J. Leverette. Requests for permission should be directed to the above address.

Trademarks: Registered trademarks of Ted J. Leverette: "Partner" On-Call, "Partner" On-Call Network, The Street-Smart Way to Buy a Business, Business Buyer Advocate, Business Buyer Protection Report, Partner On-Call Logo, BIZFIZBO, bestbusinessesforsaleonly.com.

Disclaimer: The information herein is not complete; it is intended only to provide guidelines to supplement counsel from qualified professional advisors. It is distributed with the understanding that the author, publisher and distributor are not rendering legal, accounting or tax advice or opinions on specific facts or matters, and accordingly, they assume no liability in connection with its use. Publisher, distributor and author make no warranties, expressed or implied.

Softcover ISBN: 978-1-7370119-0-3
eBook ISBN: 978-1-7370119-1-0
Library of Congress Control Number: 2021907079

Cover & Interior Design: Fusion Creative Works

Partner On-Call Network, LLC can connect you to speakers for your events.

Printed in the United States of America

Praise from Readers

Pay attention business buyers—the strategies in this book will allow you to make a great acquisition and keep you from getting a serious case of buyer fever.

— **John Martinka, author,** *Buying a Business*
That Makes You Rich

Don't forget the importance of timing. The longer you spend looking, the more it costs you, especially if you need the income.

— **Richard Parker, Diomo Corporation,**
The Business Buyer Resource Center ™

Filled with great tips for business buyers, gained from a long career of assisting buyers and sellers of hundreds of businesses. I would add one more business buying don't: Don't buy a business without reading this book.

— **Steven Beal, MBA, CGA, CFA, CBV, CBI, BEAL**
Business Brokers & Advisors

Ted's advice on creative dealmaking is second to none. If you're going to buy a business to protect your family's future, this book is insurance you'll be glad you invested in.

— **David Barnett, Author, Speaker, Educator,**
Business Buy/Sell Process Coach

Having been an intermediary for 28 years, I can honestly say that I have never encountered a more thorough presentation. I have experienced many buyers' self-destruction due to their lack of knowledge–knowledge that is in Ted's book.

— **Loren Marc Schmerler, President and Founder,**
Bottom Line Management, Inc.

I bought this book for my know-it-all spouse because we cannot afford to lose our life savings. Mission accomplished!

— **Undisclosed, to protect the innocent.**

I guess I am the kind of person your book says is all study but no action. What I like most about your book, which differentiates it from the other how-to books, is the fact that your book is not stuffed with filler (basically useless text that fills pages but cannot be put to practical use). Thanks to what your book has empowered me to do I'm getting off the dime to begin my search for a business to buy.

— **Carl Jefferson, soon-to-be-a-business owner.**

As a business broker for over 35 years, I have seen most of the dos and don'ts that are described in this book, which buyer prospects tend to make. If the buyers who come to my office read this book first, it will make my job of helping them find a business to buy much easier.

— **Jeffrey D. Jones, ASA, CBA, CBI, NACVA, Advanced Business Brokers**

Ted Leverette has definitely seen it all. His book gives you the benefit of his many years of experience and wisdom.

— **Erin Austin, Esq., Independent General Counsel**

This is an absolute gem! Every business person looking to expand their wealth by buying a business MUST read this book. Once you have read it you will always keep it in your back pocket as your quick reference guide.

— **Karl Tettmann author & architect of the GROWTH ™ Technique and Validation Principle**

If you have wanted to own your own business but are reluctant to pursue one due to the bad press about business failures and because you don't know what you don't know about the process, this is the book for you. It guides you through the steps in an easily understood and exciting way. After reading the first chapter you will feel enthusiasm for the prospect of having control of your business life, and you may lose any trepidation you may have about diving in. The book is arranged so you can efficiently browse the chapters that you need at the time you need them. It is written so well it is fun to read straight through because it gives you a helpful overview before you actually begin to look for your future business. If you want to take the pain out of looking for a business, you need this book.

— **Grace Salem, refuge from hi-tech.**

These are some of the very best caveats and recommendations to help smooth out a business buying journey—all laid out in a concise, common sense, readable fashion. They reflect the valuable combined wisdom and experience of leading experts in their field. A must-read for anyone contemplating buying a business or franchise, and a nice companion for all advisors in the dealmaking arena who want to protect their clients. So readable it will appeal even to buyers of small Main Street businesses!

— **Fayaz Karim, BSc, MBA, CPA**

Fulfilling dreams of financial independence strikes all of us as a worthwhile goal. Ted Leverette's book on buying a small or mid-size business gives us a comprehensive roadmap to get there with a thorough to do list and maybe more importantly a don't do list. This handbook could be used by an experienced buyer to fine tune their skills or by a novice to reach their first success. Enjoyable for reading or skimming and cross referenced to be immediately useful, Ted's book should be a noteworthy reference for all.

— **Louis A. Rader, retired MBA from a Fortune 500 company.**

Schizophrenic reaction. Your first chapter—'What's Possible?'—kept me in your book much longer than I intended when I began reading it. As I read the rest of your book, I went from being nervous to being excited about the possibilities. Your candid writing style, while sometimes scary, is also comforting because I want to know what is in the real world. Your book gives me the courage to begin my search for a business to buy. I'm going to form the team you recommend, and tell them about your book. Thank you, Mr. Leverette.

— **P. J. Wallace, business buyer.**

More reviews appear on partneroncall.com

Contents

Preface

You can't buy it if you can't find it.

How to Prepare Yourself and Find the Right Business to Buy—Dos, Don'ts & Profit Strategies can help you turn your business ownership dream into a wonderful reality. But buyer beware.

I wouldn't be here today if I didn't almost lose all my money after I quit my fabulous job to buy the right business the wrong way. After wasting a year trying to unscramble that rotten egg, and suing the seller for misrepresentation (and winning the lawsuit), I devoted myself to learning how to value and buy the right businesses the right ways. Since then I've enjoyed twenty eight successful small and midsize company investments.

Those experiences, and advising clients for more than thirty years, enables me to inform and guide buyers of small and midsize businesses so they can be the first choice of brokers and sellers. And avoid or beat their buyer competition. And make more-profitable done deals sooner with less aggravation at lower cost in the USA, Canada, Australia and the U.K.

If you're not sure you know everything you need to know so you can safely and profitably proceed from identifying what appears to be one or more potential acquisitions, read my other book:

- *How to **Buy** the Right Business the Right Way.*

The sale and purchase of businesses seems like a good idea for sellers and buyers until things go wrong.

The first thing to understand is sellers and their advisors do not tell buyers enough of what buyers need to know to make informed decisions about buying or investing in companies.

The second thing you need to know is neither will any of your individual advisors. You need a team to safely and profitably buy or sell a small or midsize business. You must effectively participate on your team, such as gathering how-to information on your own, such as the content of this book.

What you don't know *you don't know* can hurt you.

This book can supplement what you know about buying and selling small and midsize companies. This book can be one of your best references.

Who can benefit from these books?

- *How to **Prepare** Yourself and **Find** the **Right** Business to **Buy***

- *How to **Buy** the Right Business the Right Way?*

If you are a professional advisor, business broker or other kind of intermediary involved in mergers, acquisitions or dispositions, this book can increase your effectiveness and enable your clients to achieve safer, more profitable done deals.

If you want to buy or sell a company, this book is for you. Use it in collaboration with your dealmaking advisory team.

If you are a student or early in your career wanting to know more about what actually occurs during real-world dealmaking, this book showcases what I and my associates have witnessed over four decades—the good, bad and ugly.

Read my how-to books. And then let me help you deploy my proven best practices.

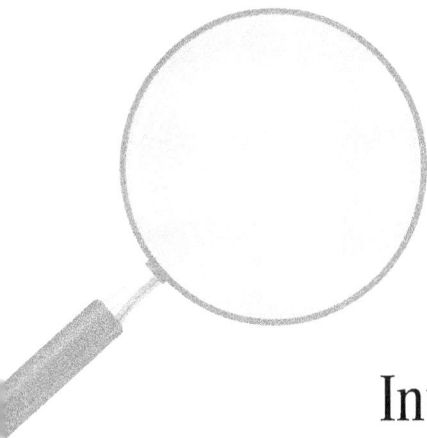

Introduction

This book (and my other book, *How to Buy the Right Business the Right Way*) is the companion to my creative financing book, *How to Get ALL the Money You Want For Your Business Without Stealing It* ™. Buying the *right* business the *right* way is more about research and analysis than negotiating and dealmaking. The more effective your due diligence the stronger will be your advantages during negotiations and dealmaking, and the easier it will be to obtain acquisition financing.

Some of the "Don'ts" in this book are more dangerous than others.

Too many of them, which individually do not pose substantial risk, by their multitude can undermine the marketability or valuation of any business and threaten *its* future and *your* investment.

There can be worthwhile opportunity with businesses for sale that are plagued by some of the problems among our "Don'ts."

If you are certain you can fix what present management did not or could not fix, you have a negotiating edge to get better terms from the seller and you can profit more from your investment. (Don't tell the seller your fix-it plan.)

This is <u>not</u> the kind of book that is best read cover-to-cover.

It's a compendium of tips, facts and strategies, any one of which if used or ignored could pivot a pending buy/sell transaction toward success or failure. As such, you can save time and more quickly find what you need by browsing the list of topics.

We are intentionally redundant on some topics.

It's necessary because we want you to be aware of certain dos, don'ts and profit strategies when your business acquisition activity is occurring during particular phases. The most common phases are shown by this book's chapter titles.

Chapter 1

What's Possible?

This chapter also appears in my other book: *How to Buy the Right Business the Right Way*. If you already read that book, you can skip this chapter. (Unless you want a reminder.)

A huge wave of mature, profitable small and midsize businesses will become available for purchase over the next decade as baby boomers convert their business equity into cash. This chapter shows you how good it can be for you.

Can you hear it? Listen . . . It's happening all around you! It's the sighs of sorrow, the worried thoughts of people, millions of them, who are seeing their earning power, and perhaps their net worth, declining because of the Great Recession, inflation, taxation, loss of job, fear of losing their job, or their dead-end job. Going from upper to middle class or from middle class to lower middle class, or worse.

What does your future look like? It depends on the decisions you make today.

You got an education. You have work experience. You've read books, listened to friends, probably attended seminars. But, perhaps like most people, you don't have what you want. Not enough of it. And you won't get it either—unless you do something about it.

Right now, right this moment, you might say to yourself, "I have had it with what I've been doing. It hasn't gotten me what I want, where I want to be. As of this moment, this very moment, I have decided to do something about it. I am done waiting. I will put to use what I learn from Ted Leverette, immediately! I haven't given up! I want more!"

Okay, did you make that decision? If so, this book is for you. You have made the decision that empowers you to become what you want to be. And, like all decisions, you can change your mind. You can decide to go back to where you were before you made that decision. You know what's waiting for you there.

So, if you didn't decide to put to use what you learn from me immediately, now's your chance. If you can't decide now, you won't get as much value from me.

I wrote this book (and I consult with clients) to help them become a bigger winner. "Winning" to me means getting what you want. You're a winner if you wake up every morning excited about the day ahead and you're delighted to be doing what you're doing, even if you're sometimes a little nervous and scared.

Have you ever said: "I'd love to have my own business?" Or, "I'd love to have my own business but I don't know how to find one or avoid making mistakes." How about this? "I'd love to have my own business but I don't think I have enough money to start or buy one."

Good. You're reading the right book. I'm going to show you how it is possible to buy a good business. An established, profitable one that pays you at least as much as you are accustomed to earning, immediately upon buying it, and more later if you improve it. The business will pay for itself—it will return your down payment (if you made one) and it will make the installment payments on its purchase, using techniques employed by tens of thousands of business owners.

It's ironic that in this land of opportunity, where so many people dream of having their own business, so little is known outside sophisticated financial circles of *how* to turn those dreams into a pleasant reality. It's a shame, too, because all the time 15-20% of businesses are for-sale (or would be in response to the right kind of inquiry). Granted, few of them are advertised for sale, especially the winners, but they *are* for-sale to people who *know* how to find and buy them.

Getting rich or *getting* control of your worklife is fun! It's more fun than being rich or in control. That's why we'll start with a game. Pretend that someone is giving you $1,000, no strings attached. What will you do with it? How will you enjoy it? Right now, imagine spending that $1,000. Have fun!

Did you spend it to buy a new toy or take a weekend vacation? Have a boisterous night on the town?

Now suppose that someone gave you $10,000. If $10,000 is small change to you, make it $50,000. If $50,000 is small change to you, you don't need to read this book! What would you do with this money? Think about it. Most people say they would put it in the bank for the bank to manage, or invest in a mutual fund for the fund to manage. This is MISTAKE #1.

Do not give other people your money to manage. Learn how to invest your own money, or at least become much more informed about investing and become more involved with your money managers.

MISTAKE #2 is a consumer mentality. If you imagined spending the money, you may have a nice toy or experience, but you won't have the money. And you won't have what the money can do for you.

If you want to progress, you must concentrate on how you can put your savings, or borrowing power, to work for you—to make more money. And to continue doing this until you have all you want. This is the single concept that separates the people who have lots of money from those who don't.

- Keep reading—I'm going to show you how to put your money to work, even as little as $1,000!

MISTAKE #3 is to believe in the fallacy of: "Find a need and fill it." That's too risky. It suggests starting a business. Savvy people find a profitable business and buy it. Remember what happened to the pioneers and settlers. The pioneers had a great idea, and while they were trying to prove it, they got arrows in their back. Later, the settlers moved in and built this country.

Buying a business is a once-in-a-lifetime experience for most people. In fact, it probably will be a once-in-a-lifetime experience if you do it wrong. You're reading this book to learn more about how to make a safe, profitable investment. You've already taken the biggest step toward getting what you want: You want to *know* how to do it. This distinguishes you from the know-it-alls and do-it-yourselfers that, according to the IRS and SBA, lose their money 80% of the time. *They* don't know what they're doing; that's why they fail.

So, let's cut to the chase. Do you have all the money you want? Do you have all the control you want?

I'm reminded of a "Peanuts" cartoon strip that showed Charlie Brown playing with half a yo-yo. It was broken. But he was having a good time dangling it, bouncing it up and down, and playing fetch with his dog Snoopy. Suddenly Charlie Brown's girlfriend Lucy comes along: "You stupid dummy," she says, "You can't have a good time with half a yo-yo. Everybody knows that!" Poor, dejected Charlie Brown throws his toy to the ground. "I'm sorry," he says, "I didn't know I couldn't enjoy myself with a broken yo-yo."

This story has a moral for people who want to quit their job and buy a business. And for people who don't want you to do so; depressing types, like the Lucys of the world who convince people that taking control is bad. They want us to feel guilty for having it or wanting it. They want to stand in our way of getting it, of discovering it is FUN TO HAVE IT. The only thing bad is not having enough of it, when you need it, like when you retire or send the kids to college or pay medical bills or simply to enjoy life.

For most people, buying a business may be the only practical way to safely and predictably increase net worth to the figure that is necessary to support themselves during retirement in a lifestyle that is comparable to what they enjoyed during their working years.

Why can't you save your way to financial security? First, you work for someone else who gets the profit on your labor. Second, the dollars you do manage to squeeze out of your overstretched budget are after-tax dollars. It is the combined forces of working for wages and the taxes on wages that make it impossible for 95% of the population to become financially secure.

Don't think there's much hope investing in stocks, bonds and most real estate. The commissions you pay middlemen greatly reduce your profit. Over the past 100 years, these types of investments generated an average annual return of approximately 10%. Take whatever money you have now and forecast out 20, 30 years at 10% growth—BEFORE-tax and BEFORE inflation. It won't work! Especially if another Great Recession arises.

One of the reasons business owners do better is they accumulate assets with PRE-tax dollars. They live on the business, taking advantage of tax loopholes designed to give them an advantage over the wage earner. And when they sell their company, the savvy small and midsize business owners continue to have the company pay for their health and life insurance, and other benefits, in PRE-tax dollars. It's part of their sale and purchase agreement.

Do you know I fly first class, stay in the best hotels, in the best rooms, eat at the best restaurants, and I'm taken around towns either in a limo or in an expensive rental car? Because I am in business, and I pay for these luxuries in PRE-tax dollars, it doesn't cost me any more money than you spend to live economy class in AFTER-tax dollars!

For readers in the USA, (at the time this book is written) do you realize we get to write-off 100% of the purchase price on a business? We get to write-off the entire price! Even goodwill! Is this an invitation to make money, or what?

Do you know that small business owners get to shelter a big chunk of profit by putting it into their own pension plans? And the earnings in the pensions are not taxable until it is withdrawn?

And, please, don't fall for the get-rich-quick magicians on social media and late night TV who promise riches from buying businesses using none of your money. Or investing in real estate or foreclosures, MLM or the "next big thing." Thousands of people have wasted their time and money chasing these pipe dreams. Sure, it is possible to make big money those ways, but it is rare for two reasons: First, too many investors are bidding on the few good properties and second, the good old days of significant appreciation are over. Think about it—name ONE wealthy person you know or have read about, other than claimed by the get-rich-quick tycoons, who is getting richer, right now doing the deals they tout. Now name 10 of them.

Compare this to the 23 MILLION privately owned businesses in the USA.

Roughly, 3 MILLION of them have made their owners wealthy. I'm not talking about the companies with 25, 50, 1000 employees, with millions of dollars invested in buildings and equipment. I'm talking about businesses with fewer than 20 employees, most with fewer than 10 employees. Go online. Look it up. These statistics are easy to confirm. Try to confirm the get-rich-quick promoters' claims!

I'm going to show you how easy it is to make a decision to get *your fair share of the wealth*. Yes, I said *easy* to make your decision. But it's hard work to do it. It takes knowledge. And, it usually takes some money—unless you *know* how to do no-money down deals (and you can find a cooperative seller of a worthwhile company).

The best deals are the ones you go out and find yourself. Not prepackaged "no-work, no worry" deals all wrapped up in a red ribbon. Where all you do is write a check. Where the red ribbon ties you up in financial knots.

Remember the Red Ribbon Rule:

If a deal sounds too good to be true, it *is* too good to be true.

You didn't just fall off the truck. You're not a fool. You know you can't pick money from trees. You already know whether or not your rich uncle is going to leave you millions when he dies. You know being a wage-slave makes the big money for somebody else.

Take a break. Right now. Figure out the amount by which your net worth must increase to make you (more) financially secure.

How much do you expect your personal net worth to increase after buying a business? In 3 years? In 7 years?

You must *know* this because it is the target return your investment in a business should produce, just as you would want to know from your stockbroker before investing in a security.

A while back, a client met the owner of a business doing $3,500,000 a year in sales. The company was started in 1910. It was being run by the grandson of the deceased founder. The grandson started putting lots of the business' profits up his nose. The business could afford his drug habit, but it could not afford his lack of attention to business while he was high. Profits were declining. Employees were jumping ship because they saw their future was at risk. My client saved the day.

He had two things the owner desperately needed: (1) He wasn't a drug addict, and (2) He knew how to manage and grow a business. My client got 51% control of this business without purchasing even 1% of the stock. He owned 51% of the stock if he stopped the company from losing ground. Not grow, but simply stop the slide. Why would the seller agree to this? Because he was faced with losing it all.

Why could my client get this opportunity? Because he knew how.

It is not easy to find one of these deals. In fact, without a very specific *search system* it's nearly impossible to find one. And when you find one, you must *know* exactly what to do, in the *correct sequence*. You must act very quickly, or somebody else gets the deal.

Do you have more than $500,000 cash for the down payment to buy a business? $250,000 to $350,000? $100,000 to $200,000? Nothing?

Would you like to buy a business for 1/4 to 1/3 its price? First a distinction. There's a difference between buying and paying. You buy the company. The company pays most of the price. Here's how it's done:

You make the typical cash down payment of 1/4 to 1/3 the price. The balance is paid in installments from the business' profit. (You should never dip into your pockets to make the payments.) Therefore, your investment in the business is your down payment. So, it's easy to buy for less than the price; make a small down payment to buy a profitable business. Think about it. The seller is delighted because he sold his business and he gets a nice income from the buyer for many years. This is no different from the apartment building owner who makes a down payment and lets the tenants pay off the mortgage and return the owner's down payment, so one day he owns the building free and clear.

What if you don't have the full down payment? You need money to make money, but it doesn't have to be *your* money.

If you don't have enough cash, use OPM, other people's money. OPM comes from lenders and investors. It also comes from refinancing the business you buy. You can't use OPM unless you know how. We're talking about the concept of leverage and milking the company's cash flow: Adding what you know about getting money to the money you have.

Important tip: The best OPM isn't borrowed. There are two problems with borrowing. (1) You have to pay it back, maybe before you can or want to, and (2) you have to pay interest for it, on a payment schedule that may get in your way of using the business' cash for other purposes, like to make more money.

The best OPM comes from investors. These people do not expect short-term payments and profit as do lenders. These people advance more money to you if you give them a greater share of your profits. If the business is not profitable, they don't get a return on their investment, just as you don't. If the business is a bust, they lose money. If you bought the street-smart way, your cash investment was so low that you got it back from operating the business before it had a chance to go bust. You don't even lose the value of your time, because you make sure the business pays you a management wage as you go along, right up to the day you fold your tent and find another business to run.

Do you realize most worthwhile companies bring in enough cash in one month to cover the down payment? There is no rule that says you can't use some of those dollars. You just have to know how.

Your lack of capital can be a handicap, but it needn't be an obstacle!

Would your life be better if you had more money? More control? How would it be?

Imagine this:

You want to own a winner business, to earn money based upon your performance, not what the boss doles out to you, to control your worklife, to feel financially and emotionally secure because you are doing exactly what you want . . . to wake up every morning excited about the day ahead and delighted with the life you made for yourself. Imagine your status in your community when you have this. Imagine your status in your own family.

This book (and a good business acquisition advisory team) can show you many ways to make money, to get control. Knowledge is power. This book contains facts, tips, strategies and examples, any one of which can accelerate your success, if you put your knowledge to work. This is what you want, isn't it?

Here's what Barbara Williams told me: "I had trouble believing what you said, that I could think my way out of failure. Until I realized it was my own self-limiting thoughts that made me what I was. As long as I kept trying to believe in myself and reform my bad habits, I kept crashing, and blaming myself. It was not until I gave up on fixing me and started using your tools that I discovered that I could succeed, despite myself."

J. Paul Getty, one of the richest men in the world, said there are three steps to getting what you want: Set specific goals. Learn strategies to achieve them. Implement your plan.

Does this make sense to you?

Stop right here.

- Is this book causing you to become more excited about owning a company or growing your company via acquisitions and mergers? If you're a professional advisor or a business broker, or maybe a business seller, is what you are reading so far too much feel-good news? Let's take a break. Mark this page. And then look for a dozen or so topic headings in this book that begin with the word, "Don't." Doing so will show you that buying a business is not peaches and cream, a walk in the park—you know what I mean. But, please do not (yet) read topics that do not begin with the word, "Don't." Save those for after coming back to this page and finishing this chapter. Trust me. I know what I'm doing with this request.

Okay, you're back. Thank you.

Let's exercise your imagination because, as Wynn Davis says, "Seeing all the possibilities, seeing all that can be done, and how it can be done, marks the power of imagination. Our imagination is our own personal laboratory. Here we can recreate events, map plans, and visualize overcoming obstacles. Imagination shows us how to turn possibility into reality."

Why would anybody sell a winner? Mark this page, and then find and read this topic in this book: "Owner's catastrophe signals your buying opportunity." And then come back here.

Thinking about turning around a loser? Mark this page again, and then find and read this topic in this book: "Don't buy a loser." And then come back here. (I mean it.)

You must *want* to own a business.

Abraham Maslow, the visionary psychologist, said, "All we are likely to learn from dwelling on what doesn't work in life is to be an expert at what doesn't work."

He observed that "people who continually get what they want continually take action, the purpose of which is to take them from where they are to where they want to be, and as they progress, their action provides them with an unfolding, joyful experience of their personal power.

He went on to report that if we are in an environment that supports our evolution toward self-actualization, then it will happen, and if we are not, then it won't happen."

He said, "If we fail to recognize this principle and apply it, and persist in seeing ourselves as victims of an environment over which we have no control, then we will lead a colorless existence as members of the living dead."

And what Maslow said next is what caused me to write this book for you:

"The only way out is to be inspired out; in other words, to have a direct experience of someone who is living from a reality that is outside the no-fun and incomplete life so many people live."

He said, "The people who are making it in life are making it *and* they have fear. The people who are not making it *just* have fear.

Stewart Emery said, "Somehow people have the notion that they are going to get away from failure, that they are going to succeed enough never to fail again. That option is simply not available; it is like trying to eat once and for all."

We have observed that up to 50% of sellers (depending upon the industry and size of company) back out of deals because they are not confident the potential buyer knows how to buy a business or because the seller is not sure the buyer can properly manage the business. Why? Because it is typical, in today's post-Great Recession marketplace, for sellers to fear that buyers won't pay off the entire seller financing. And some "sellers" string along unsuspecting buyers, so they can practice selling their business while getting free management advice from the buyers.

Does it have to be this way? Absolutely not! You can choose not to take the typical course. A thoughtful analysis of this situation reveals that much of this wasted time and money is the result of buyers committing errors in the following areas, all of which you control:

- First impression. The best companies for sale are typically mishandled by searchers/buyers during the first seller contact. There are two sales being made from the first moment. The seller is trying to sell you his business and you are trying to sell yourself. (Remember, you're effectively applying for the job of company president.)

- Resume. Either buyers don't know or they ignore the importance of furnishing sellers their credentials during their first meeting. Or worse, what they show is improperly constructed. The resume's format and content, which people use while looking for a job, will not appropriately showcase the *business buyer's* credentials.

- Team. Searchers approaching sellers without identifying their experienced acquisition team invite sellers to wonder whether the buyer would also try to manage the business as a one-man-show.

- Money. Searchers should KNOW how to present their financial capability. Showing too much cash and net worth increases the probability of paying too much and making a larger than necessary down payment. Or being rejected by sellers when searchers refuse to use more of their money.

Searchers revealing too little may not get a chance to evaluate the company.

- Criteria. Searchers/buyers are wasting time looking at businesses too large or too small in relation to their buying and management capabilities.

- Search method. A faulty search mostly produces losers. The few winners which are found are not accessible because the seller's asking terms are not reasonable (except to the naive buyer).

The only thing that stands between a man
and what he wants from life is often merely the will to
try it and the faith to believe that it is possible.

— Richard M. DeVos

Most of the wealth in this country was created by people who knew how to use money. Think about it. The only mysterious thing about how *they* do it is what *you* do not know about it.

To buy at or below Fair Market Value (FMV) you must do two things: Learn how to do it, and then do some of the work yourself. If you rely on a broker, or anyone else, to do too much of the work, some or all of your potential gain will be earned by them.

- To be clear: Savvy buyers employ an acquisition advisory team, and those buyers are actively involved in the process; they do not sit on the sidelines waiting for reports from advisors.

The job or company you have now, and your present risk, is no less than what you'd have if you implemented my techniques to make more money.

Either you're buying a business for yourself or you're effectively buying one for your employer. The profit your employer earns on your labor creates value for his or her company. What are you left with? Not much! Certainly not enough to live the lifestyle you want or to be financially secure when you retire. Isn't that right?

Are you working hard to help somebody else own a company that creates their financial security? Isn't this risky, if you're not paid enough to save enough; if you can be fired and the company can go out of business if management can't do its job?

I want to show you what works. Start by setting a target date. It's the antidote to both procrastination ("Oh, I'll get to it someday") and despair ("I'll never get there").

The sooner you start getting more of what you really want, the more energy you'll have for the rest of it!

The most difficult step any of us take is the first one, when we rise to our feet against all the protests of our inner selves and then proceed to do something that we know we ought to do. Our very soul may squirm, but we will be acting the part of someone who is going to make more money.

— Norman Vincent Peale

Buy, don't start, a business.

Buying a business is usually cheaper, faster, safer and more profitable than starting one. By purchasing a business, you don't add to the competition. You get a business' profit—from day one. When you start a business, however, the cash flow is from your pocket out the door. Think about it. If you do a startup, you go into competition with everyone else in the industry. If you can buy cheaper, why start? There's another reason not to start a business. Most of them fail! Buy an existing winner if you want to win.

What if the seller owns the building, in which the business operates? It's rarely feasible or smart to buy the building.

Three problems:

1. It may require a large cash down payment on the value of the building for a bank to finance the balance. You may not have enough money for a down payment on the building *and* for the business.

2. Good management of a business creates a much larger return on investment than is possible from owning commercial real estate, especially now.

3. If your business is hit by a cash flow crisis, you will have to find a way to make the mortgage payment; otherwise the building can be foreclosed upon. If you don't pay suppliers, so you can pay the mortgage, they may refuse to ship to you except COD. If you don't pay employees, they may quit or their morale erodes. Of course, you don't have to pay yourself, but how will you feed the family?

There's a better way, the street-smart way: Tell the seller to keep the building and you will lease it from him. He can get a mortgage against it if he really needs cash. You can use a lease with an option to purchase, say in five years when you can afford it. Or, he can sell it to a real estate investor who becomes your landlord.

Important concept: Look to the assets of the business itself to raise the cash for the down payment (or to recoup your down payment). Use the business' cash flow to make payments to whatever sources provided you with money for the down payment, and to pay the seller for the balance of the price that the seller financed.

You should not use more of your money than necessary, even if you have lots of money. This minimizes your risk in the event of a disaster and it can increase your return on investment.

Your upside far exceeds your downside if you buy a good business on the right terms.

Example of how good it can be.

John used the techniques I taught him. He bought a forty-year old manufacturer of patented low-tech industrial products. The elderly man who was selling the company invented some of the products. These products do not become obsolete. All of the company's revenue came from repeat business and word-of-mouth among customers. He hadn't made a sales call in years. He had no catalog or brochure. No marketing effort whatsoever. We noticed that the company's products were only sold in the U.S. We asked if there was demand for them abroad. The owner said there was but he never got around to looking into it because he didn't want to put up with all the paperwork necessary to export and do business with foreigners.

Here's what my client, John, did. Within ninety days of buying the company, he launched a national marketing blitz. He established dealers across the country. (Before then, the company sold direct to customers.) He furnished dealers with four-color marketing materials. He sent them a video showing how to install and service the products. Within five months, he was selling internationally. Within six months, the company's profits had doubled, from $20,000 per month to $40,000 per month; that's nearly $500,000 per year! Around that time, he got his first offer to buy his business from a large company that had been watching this sleepy little firm take off like a rocket ship.

John was an experienced businessman. He knew how to run and grow companies. But he was not an expert in buying them. And, he recognized that even if he knew how to buy, he first had to find a winner. My *Business-For-Sale Locating & Screening System* ™ enabled him to see dozens of companies. He cherry-picked the winner he bought from several other winners. Would you like to do that?

Let's kill myths.

"It takes money to make money."

True, but it doesn't have to be your money.

"A penny saved is a penny earned."

So what! What can a penny buy?

It becomes a dollar when you wisely invest it.

"It's *whom* you know, not what you know."

Savvy people say: It's who *knows you* that counts.

"Work hard, not smart pays poorly and is no fun."

Work smart, not hard gets better than average results.

Work smart and work hard gets extraordinary results.

"Ah, come on Ted. You say to use other people's money. I believe I can borrow it, if I use the business' assets or profit as collateral. But get it from investors? I don't think so."

Would you be interested if I could show you that it *is* possible to get money from investors? Would *knowing* this help you see that you can own a business if you learn how to find a winner and if you learn how to buy it the right way? Well, here it goes:

At some point successful people are so busy managing the business they own, or the company they run for somebody else, that they don't have time for anything else. They are out of time, but they are not out of money. Every month their stockpile of money grows from their business and investment profits. What can they do with this cash? Invest in the stocks and bonds of publicly traded companies? Sure. Possibly real estate? Maybe, though that's not expected to be the best investment for a while.

Affluent people got that way by being smart. They know to spread the risk, to diversify their investments. So, they put some money in safe, publicly traded securities. They earn, if they're well-invested, maybe 10% per year on this money. Some they put in higher risk stocks, but not too much, because they can be crushed by institutional investors, hedge funds and Wall Street investment bankers who easily manipulate these stocks.

Some people who want to make more than 10% on their money, and are willing to take a bigger risk to get it, invest in small, private companies. Companies where somebody else has their life on the line, trying to make it grow. The well-off investor's strategy is: "Their brains and sweat, my money."

They want you to bring them deals, companies you have packaged for acquisition. They tell you their investment criteria, so you know what to look for. You'll like what they like, because they want to make money, and they know how to specify moneymaking businesses. They won't give you all their money, not even a lot of it. It depends on how much cash they have available when you present your proposal. And it depends on the company and its potential for profit.

Is it easy to find these people? Yes. You can find them by searching online. They are on LinkedIn and other social media. They are featured in the news. You know the neighborhoods in which they live, the clubs to which they belong. Finding is easy. Convincing them to listen to you is hard. When you know how to correctly present your offer to them, they listen and you have a chance at their money. I've shown thousands of people how to find money. I've been a provider of money myself.

Most people have a distorted notion of how things actually get done in this world. Great deeds are made up of small, steady actions. You know—the longest journey is made in small steps. I'm in the business of showing the steps to people, and helping people step forward.

Now, here are three questions for you:

1. Are you seeing how having the right advisory team can help you save time and money, make more money and reduce your risk?

2. Are you interested in more money and less risk?

3. If you want to make more money and have greater control over your work life, when is the best time to start?

Company sellers start with advantages over you.

You must level the playing field.

You do know, don't you, that sellers have professional advisors to help them make the sale and to protect them from you?

Do you understand that whether or not you want to be, if you proceed alone you will be your own "professional" advisor?

Do you feel knowledgeable enough to find the winners, and then thoroughly investigate the company and then negotiate a deal with the seller and his experts?

You probably have as high a regard for your money as sellers do for theirs.

Do you realize the seller and his advisors' job is to get the most money from you and to do as little as possible to make sure you make a smart investment? (This is not to suggest sellers will lie to you, although they might omit to tell you something if you don't know to ask.)

Can you afford the time, money and aggravation it would take for you to have a deal fall apart because you could not get the seller to agree to your terms, and then you must start over sifting through all the loser businesses to find another winner?

It's been said that nobody who has failed complains that they got too much useful advice.

Deals are happening around you every day, and each one you miss costs you money. The window of opportunity is open, but maybe not for long.

Get started right.

One of the most crucial things in searching for a company to buy is to get started right. You only have one chance to make a favorable first impression. If you don't have all the components in place before you meet the owner of a good business, you could blow your chance to buy it.

It comes down to this: I don't know your dreams, but most people say they need more money or more control over their worklife. Some people need big money, to put their kids through college or to fund their retirement. Others want to be rich(er). Some people simply want to have more spending money, and are willing to work hard to get it.

What's it worth to you to know how to find the right business and to know what to do when you find it?

What's it worth to you to make the amount of money you want, and to control your worklife?

What's it worth to you to finally become what you've dreamed?

What's it worth to you to be able to do it now, by taking steps that others have perfected over the years?

This book can be one of the tools that help you achieve the success you seek.

But don't let do-it-yourself thinking slow you down or increase your risk. Why risk everything by trying to cut a few corners or by isolating yourself from the street-smart experience of a business acquisition advisory team whose sole purpose is to protect you and to maximize your profit?

Imagine you are taking up skydiving. You attend a pre-jump lecture, and then learn how to pack your parachute.

Would you say this to the instructor? "Thanks for the lecture on how to pack my chute, jump and then land. See ya later!" And then board the airplane by yourself? Flash to reality. Wouldn't you expect your instructor to accompany you on board the airplane, to build your confidence while the plane is moving into position, to encourage you to jump, and possibly to make the first jump a tandem one, where you and the expert do it together so you land safely, with both feet firmly on the ground?

Buying a business is like sky diving. It can be lots of fun or it can kill you.

This book shows how sellers and their advisors plan to sell you a business and the strategies they employ to influence you. While safely reading this book, you learn about mistakes most people make, so you don't make them in the real world with wasted time and money.

Do you remember at the start of this chapter, I told you I would show you how to put your money to work? As little as $1,000? Now I'm going to show you how to put $1,000 to work. Invest it in your business acquisition advisory team.

With the knowledge from one or more members of your team, as you get started or as you dig deeper into the deal before you, you're increasing your odds that you can make a profitable investment, and get more control over your worklife.

You could be the best carpenter in the world, but what can you build without a toolbox? This book is one of your moneymaking tools. Your business acquisition advisory team helps you implement what you read in this book, and beyond.

This book develops the big strategies; it warns you and encourages you. And it explains how to implement some of what you need to do. But it's like reading and then trying to cook a recipe. The food probably won't taste like you thought it would until several tries, if ever, even if you use the right amount of all the ingredients and use the right amount of heat for the right amount of time. It's all in the technique, the methodologies. You can practice with your time and money, or your advisory team can help you do what works.

Who's smarter? Rats or people?

If you put a chunk of cheese at one end of a maze and a rat at the other, the rat will run down the maze a few times and very quickly figure out the paths that do not lead to the cheese. Rats are quick to eliminate what doesn't work. That's why rats get the cheese. The difference between a rat and humans is most humans will continue to go down the same paths until they starve to death.

Chapter 2

One Word Distinguishes Successful Business Buyers

According to the top intermediaries and advisors, 93% of people wanting to buy or merge small or midsize companies fail to do so. Most of them don't even make it to third base.

Just one word differentiates the winners from the losers who **do** and who **don't** buy small and midsize companies.

Most people don't know what it is.

How do I know? I surveyed 10,000 people. Nearly all of them are buy/sell dealmakers or their representatives or advisors. And some of them are failing wannabes. So far, they have suggested and explained more than 60 important attributes, which can result in done deals.

One word is the common denominator: Guts!

Why do we know this? Our 500-year collective experience working for acquirers as their *Business Buyer Advocate.*

We also surveyed 10,000 people on the buy/sell playing field: Acquirers, attorneys, accountants, appraisers, brokers and sources of financing. We also communicated with failing wannabes.

The MOST important attribute may not be what you think it is.

And guess what? Most of the people, proposing the one word, were wrong. Not my opinion; theirs, after I explained the rationale for the MOST important characteristic.

What some of us believe to be the *most* indispensable characteristic may upset the usual thinking of some people, including professional advisors.

First of all, winners actually achieve done deals. And that happens because they stay the course. This happens because they bring to the dealmaking playing field as many or more than 60 attributes, just one of which empowers everything else. If that one attribute, guts, is missing or weak, people probably won't buy a business.

This information can educate people who want to achieve a done deal; it can also help their advisors. Advisors? Sure. Winning professional reputations are made when advisors enable clients to succeed. Advisors make more money from clients that progress all the way to a done deal. Some of you can use my books for your self-assessment.

Why is this important? I don't know anyone who wants to fail. Do you? And too many people fail because they don't have what it takes for success.

People who buy or merge small and midsize companies have some or all of certain characteristics, traits, attitudes, qualifications.

People who are best at coping with and overcoming their inertia and their fears smooth their pathway to buying a business. When their gut tells them to push through resistance or to solve a problem, they're not afraid to try. Knowing how to overcome fear is what permits us to fully release our potential. Because we have the guts to do it.

All of these personality characteristics are important. One of them, guts, is the *most* important, for without it people are not likely to achieve done deals.

Use this chapter to evaluate what you bring to the table. And then showcase your strengths when you interact with people on your way to achieving a done deal. Get help from your advisory team to shore up your deficiencies.

The relative benefits and importance will change for each of these characteristics as you progress. But, remember: Underlying all of them is the *indispensable* one; nourish it. Guts!

Ask yourself this question about any of the traits we review in this book:

- If I have X but not the *most* indispensable one, am I more likely or not to buy a business?

As an example, here's a tip you can use to test each of the attributes. It is an example of an important attribute. But it is *not* the most important one.

- "Desire" (i.e., to want something very strongly). Sure, desire is a universal attribute, but is there any other characteristic, trait or behavior that, if *missing*, will not permit *desire* to prevail? Which attribute, if lacking, will ultimately dissolve the best of intentions?

You can apply the test, above, to any of the characteristics this book lists. This list shows the complexity of what comes to play. These attributes, for each potential acquirer, may not be in alignment; they may not be congruent. Some of them may, indeed, be in conflict. This is normal.

Below are the names of a few people who helped me with this chapter. Anything you like about this chapter is thanks to them. Blame me for anything you don't like or don't agree with.

William P. Stubbs, Jr., Gary Hallett, Nancy Fallon-Houle, John Martinka, Jordan Westropp, Hal Janke, Nathan Edelen, Raymond Copell, Steven Beal, Bob Fariss, Lanny Moldofsky, Dean Liguori, Robert Mitchell, Eric S. Arroyo, Gregory Kovsky, Ron Hitson, Rakesh Malhotra, Jennifer Lee, William Yankee, Robert L. Kelcourse, John McGrane.

Okay, on to the list . . .

100% focus and commitment to closing the deal.

If the buyer needs to be pushed, prodded or dragged to the finish line - the deal is dead. If the buyer keeps pushing the broker, the seller, the banker, and the lawyer and accountant to get their work done to close the deal - then this deal is 25 times more likely to close than it would with a passive buyer.

Able to perceive opportunity where others do not.

The biggest OH WOW (!) is this: When you're an employee, you ARE buying a business . . . for your employer, though you may not have thought of it that way.

The profit your employer earns on your labor creates value for his business.

What are you left with?

Is it enough to live the lifestyle you want, or to be financially secure when you retire?

Sure, it's risky to buy a business. But it's also risky to be an employee, especially if you're not paid enough to save enough. You can be fired. The company can go out of business if management can't do its job. Right?

So, potential buyers (and their advisors): There are no worst types of business—but a particular business may not be worth buying. You can make a street-smart investment by acquiring a strong company in a temporarily troubled or declining industry.

Access the hidden market.

This is where to find unadvertised businesses for sale by-owner (or could be for sale to buyers who properly approach and interact with owners).

No matter how experienced you are, here are a few obstacles standing in the way of you buying a business:

There is a horde of unemployed or inexperienced buyers; they bid against each other to create a *seller's* market.

Only 1 out of 5 of the *best* companies sold are advertised by sellers or offered through business brokers.

Being qualified to buy a business is not enough. You must know how to find winners and achieve a done deal.

(As you can imagine, statistics, like these, vary depending upon the time, industry and the national and local economic conditions. You can easily Google the topic and find the array of data. When we counsel buyers, we tell them to take all stats with a large grain of salt, which means what matters most is the degree to which worthwhile companies can be found to match a particular buyer's acquisition criteria. The figure we cite, here, has been most relevant to most of the buyers who hire us. Our buyers seek small and midsize companies for sale, not Main Street ventures.)

Searching (only) in the public market is like rowing a boat with one oar; it takes a lot of effort and you don't get far.

Accurate screening.

Of people and business opportunities. Don't expect sellers and their representatives to tell you everything they know. It's up to you to know how to evaluate opportunities. And do it. Most businesses are not worth owning. Their owners hope for a naive buyer, such as a Greater Fool.

Acquisition criteria.

It's important that the criterion for target businesses is compatible with the buyer's suitability for the business.

Begin with realistic acquisition criteria.

Criteria include business type, size, age, location, customer and product diversification, degree of competition, working hours, travel requirement, etc.

A safe and profitable business acquisition pays the owner a fair salary and benefits, earns enough profit for the business to pay for itself, provides a decent return on investment and later will sell for more than the price you paid.

Alignment.

Alignment of strategic rationale, alignment of values, alignment with seller to get a win-win deal, etc.

Analytical.

Buying the right business the right way is more about research and analysis than negotiating and dealmaking. The more effective your due diligence the stronger will be your advantages during negotiations and dealmaking, and the easier it will be to obtain acquisition financing.

Too many choices can lead to paralysis (by analysis) and dissatisfaction. Too many choices cause us to waste time making decisions and worrying that we might be making mistakes. Buyer confusion can be followed by buyer remorse if the buyer imagines that a better deal was available elsewhere.

The worst case we saw was a former CEO who wasted two years to find 205 sellers (in various industries) of which 40 were excellent acquisitions. He kept postponing his decision to buy because he thought there would be a better deal down the road. The business he bought was no better than most of the winners that he saw early in his search.

Avoid toxic people.

Toxic behavior is common in the workplace, and that includes the playing field for the buying and selling of companies.

For most people, buying a business may be the only practical way to safely and predictably increase net worth to the figure that is necessary to support themselves during retirement in a lifestyle that is comparable to what they enjoyed during their working years.

Therefore, doesn't it make sense to you to shield yourself from toxic behavior? Try to limit or walk away from people who try to infect you. If it's not practical to walk away, minimize interactions. This is easier done if you're working from a well-thought-out work-plan and if you can delegate to your advisory team.

And, maybe you can try harder not to let those jerks upset you or pop your balloons (as much).

I'm reminded of a "Peanuts" cartoon strip that showed Charlie Brown playing with half a yo-yo. It was broken. But he was having a good time dangling it, bouncing it up and down, and playing fetch with his dog Snoopy. Suddenly Charlie Brown's girlfriend Lucy comes along: "You stupid dummy," she says, "You can't have a good time with half a yo-yo. Everybody knows that!" Poor, dejected Charlie Brown throws his toy to the ground. "I'm sorry," he says, "I didn't know I couldn't enjoy myself with a broken yo-yo."

Aware.

Aware of the market conditions, the risks and the opportunities, and willing to proceed.

The art of successful business ownership is more complex than simply running the company. How did the owner come by owning it? If the owner purchased the company, how and why it was acquired materially affects the degree to which it can be successfully operated. Some mistakes during the planning, searching and acquiring the company can hamstring its performance. And, there's not much company management can do about it, except to acquiesce to the reality of mediocrity or failure.

Buy for the right reasons.

According to a survey conducted by Opinion Research Inc., the desire to get rich was cited by only 9% of people who want to become a business owner.

The strongest reasons for wanting to own a business: "doing something I love" and "security."

So adept sellers and brokers showcase the *enjoyment* the company offers. They appeal to the buyer's desire to "do something I love."

Sellers and brokers stimulate the buyer's need for *security*, showing how the company can provide permanence of employment and financial security.

Safety is more important to most buyers than profit—no matter what buyers say.

Most buyers won't buy an unprofitable business, but many buyers will purchase a business whose profit has been less than the buyer initially wants if the buyer believes the business is not about to suffer a downturn.

Studies say security is the fundamental, universal reason why people want to own a business.

A "buyer" who is willing to take the risk of buying a business does so because of his/her belief that the only real security from a job is the job that he/she creates in the company he/she owns. A wise business seller subtly encourages buyers to fully understand this. Buyers who have lost or hate their job see the truth in this.

Ending or preventing unemployment is not necessarily a good reason to buy a company.

Brave.

Most people are brave if they do what it takes to achieve done deals, given the risk and danger associated with buying and merging companies.

They have courage combined with a willingness to take risks or attempt difficult or unconventional things (which, certainly, pertains to business transactions).

Antonyms for brave shed light on bravery but let's precede each antonym with this common-sense qualifier: "excessively or unreasonably." Such as excessively or unreasonably afraid, careful, cautious, unadventurous.

See also: *Guts.*

Capable acquisition advisory team.

Oh, you might wonder: Why a team? (Buying a company without professional help is about as smart as building a house without a good contractor. Do I have to give another analogy?)

The other side of the dealmaking table, sellers, has a team. And sellers employing business brokers enjoy 62 benefits, quite a few of which give them advantages over buyers.

Let's focus on **selecting your advisory team:**

- Hire people with a proven history of working for *buyers and sellers* of the kind and size of deal you intend.

- Ask how they have *facilitated* deals that *should* and *did* occur.

- Hire dealmakers, deal closers.

Avoid the *wrong* kind of deal killer. There are two kinds of deal killers:

- There are advisors who don't know enough about dealmaking for small and midsize companies. Not wanting to make mistakes these poseurs are more likely to poo-poo deals or, worse, bless them.

- The other kind of deal killer is adequately experienced, which means when they try to kill the deal, do it.

You can get a better result if all the members of your advisory have a future-focus; if they can help you discover and exploit opportunities instead of turning every potential risk into a life-threatening situation. Sure, it's important to detect vulnerabilities. And the best advisors can show you how to fix or live with them within an *already-profitable* company.

Clarity about intent.

Clarity of objectives, goals, values, price capability, etc.

- Thanks for this definition by **Jennifer Lee,** MBA.

Communication effectiveness.

Effective at listening and honest communication.

Committed to achieve a done deal.

To do what needs to be done.

Compatibility insight.

Understanding how and where the acquired company fits into the acquirer's current and future needs.

Confident about fit.

Buyers are happier when they understand, before setting out to buy or merge a company, about how and where the acquired company will fit into the buyer's current and future needs.

Consistency.

Without consistency, no traction is built up for deal flow. You aren't able to even make the first acquisition if you're not taking consistent action to put the proper systems in place. If you continue to put forth that effort it will pay off in your deal making career.

Courageous.

The one word that I believe separates the winners from the losers is courage.

Antonyms for courageous shed light on this attribute but let's precede each antonym with this common sense qualifier: "excessively or unreasonably." Such as excessively or unreasonably cowardly, irresolute, yielding, faint-hearted.

See also: *Guts.*

Creativeness.

How about creative dealmaking? This is where your team can shine for you (if you hire the right people).

How about creative financing? *How to Get ALL the Money You Want For Your Business Without Stealing It* (Choose the USA or Canadian version.)

"Ted's advice on creative dealmaking is second to none. I once helped my wife buy a business and used some of his tricks such as time-limiting personal guarantees on vendor notes. I'm glad to see this tidbit and more fill the pages of his latest book. If you're going to buy a business to protect your family's future, this book is one tiny bit of insurance you'll be glad you invested in."

Credentials.

What the buyer brings to the table must be acceptable to sellers (and probably to the sellers' advisors, and maybe to the company's customers, employees, landlord, bank and suppliers).

Too many buyers don't know or they ignore the importance of furnishing sellers, during the first meeting, their credentials, or worse, what they show is improperly constructed. The "resume's" (for lack of a better word) format and content, which people use while looking for a job, will not appropriately showcase the business buyer's credentials.

Decisive.

The ability to make decisions quickly and effectively. (You will not feel rushed to decide if you definitively explain, to sellers and their advisors, for example, how you will gather the information you need to make informed decisions.)

Keep in mind that sellers and their team are trying to figure out how you will perform if you buy the company. This is particularly important to sellers that finance part of the buyer's purchase price.

Decisiveness suggests leadership ability.

Dithering won't cut it. Neither will unreasonable hesitation.

Desire.

Buyers that go after a business the same way they would go after a potential spouse are a pleasure to work with.

Determination.

It's probably not the one word you hear most, but it is the key, according to a broker who says:

"As I call it, it's the 'get up off your ass factor.'

'When you know, or think you know, there is something you should do as a buyer (or, seller/broker/rainmaker) and you 'get up off your ass' and really do something about it, you've got the best chance of success. Success is a doing something."

Doer.

Go-getter; achiever. You have a history (way before yesterday!) of taking action instead of just thinking or talking about it. Thinking about it is good. *Only* thinking about it is not. Neither is unnecessary procrastination.

"It is not the critic who counts; not the man who points out how the strong man stumbles, or where the doer of deeds could have done better. The credit belongs to the man who is actually in the arena, whose face is marred by dust and sweat and blood; who strived valiantly; who errs, who comes again and again, because there is no effort without error and shortcoming; but who does actually strive to do the deeds; who knows great enthusiasms, the great devotions; who spends himself in a worthy cause; who at the best knows in the end the triumph of high achievement, and who at the worst, if he fails, at least fails while daring greatly."

— Teddy Roosevelt

Financially capable.

Depending upon the industry and type of buy/sell transaction—where the seller and buyer reached agreement on everything else—up to 50% failed to close due to lack of acquisition financing, according to a national survey.

So, pay attention when business brokers and other knowledgeable professionals tell you how much money and borrowing power you need to achieve the kind of deal you intend.

The buyer should KNOW how to present his financial capability. If he shows too much, he increases the probability that he will pay too much and make a larger than necessary down payment, or be rejected by the seller when he refuses to use more of his money. If he reveals too little, he will not get a chance to evaluate the company.

Buyer's credit report and creditworthiness: It takes a knowledgeable buyer or a savvy acquisition team to position the business buyer for the kinds of financial scrutiny that arises during dealmaking.

If and when buyers quit their job to buy a company can have a huge bearing on whether or not a deal can occur.

Likewise, how and when the potential buyer manipulates the buyer's finances and borrowing power.

And, let's not forget honest asset protection for buyers who don't want everything they own to be on the line.

It's amazing that so many people say their lack of money and/or borrowing power is why they don't try to achieve their dream of owning a business. More of them could do so if they deploy some of the 500 creative financing techniques in my book: *How to Get ALL the Money You Want For Your Business Without Stealing* It (Choose the USA or Canadian version.)

Future-focus.

Google, Facebook, Amazon and Apple have it because their employees, advisors and investors have it. If you don't have the proven ability to accurate perceive the future (for your company), hire people who do. ASAP!

Grit.

Grit is the strength of mind that enables a person to endure pain or hardship.

Grit is the ability that demonstrates your passion, perseverance and determination towards long term goals. This means when things get hard you push even harder; when you fail you get up stronger; when you don't see result you don't give up, you continue with relentless energy, enthusiasm, consistency, heart, soul and passion.

According to the Merriam-Webster dictionary, grit in the context of behavior is defined as "firmness of character; indomitable spirit." Angela Duckworth, based on her studies, tweaked this definition to be "perseverance and passion for long-term goals."

See also: *Guts.*

Guts!

With *enough* "guts" people actually do it; they do what it takes to achieve done deals. This requires commitment to their goal and persistence no matter what (i.e., setbacks, disappointments).

Some people prefer the phrase "intestinal fortitude," which means: staying power, stick-to-itiveness.

Reliable information fuels guts and it can dissolve fear. It's not mere conviction or resolve; those are separate attributes. People may not achieve done deals if their fear of failure overcomes their conviction or resolve. But informed courage can prevail over everything else that attempts to inhibit your progress.

Guts have to be tempered (with an advisory team, know-how, common sense, reality checks); otherwise, people can do a bad deal, such as buying the wrong business or purchasing the right one the wrong way. Being driven by guts is the *indispensable* characteristic, the *most* important one.

Having *enough* "guts" is *not* a universal attribute. Sufficient guts, if *missing*, may be what stops most people who want to buy a business, even if their opportunity is legitimately wonderful.

Guts means to have *grit, courage, bravery and daring.* Those attributes are crucial, essential and required for people who want to increase the probability that they will get what they want, especially in a risk-laden environment such as buying and merging companies.

Antonyms for guts shed light on this attribute but let's precede each antonym with this common sense qualifier: "excessively or unreasonably." Such as excessively or unreasonably chicken and unwilling.

If you have enough guts to do what it takes to achieve a done deal, nothing can stop you unless, on the basis of rationality, you decide to abort deals to pursue better deals.

First-time buyers are most likely to quit.

Do you agree that "guts," if lacking, will ultimately dissolve the best of intentions, i.e., that people are likely to fail to achieve whatever they want?

Also see: Intuition. Brave. Grit. Courage.

Honesty.

This online definition says it: Honesty refers to a facet of moral character and connotes positive and virtuous attributes such as integrity, truthfulness, straightforwardness, including straightforwardness of conduct, along with the absence of lying, cheating, theft, etc. Honestly also includes being trustworthy, loyal, fair, and sincere.

If you don't have it, do you have a good lawyer?

Human relations abilities.

This is important throughout the search and buying activities. But it's (arguably) more important when buyers transition into their company.

Hunting savvy.

Isn't finding a terrific deal a long shot?

Yes, if you make either of two mistakes:

- Limit your shopping to where all the other buyers are shopping.

- Don't know how to quickly put together a worthwhile deal.

It's important that you learn how to meet owners of the best companies for sale plus the companies that are about to be for sale—before they have a chance to list their business for sale with a broker. The longer brokers are on scene, the more time they have to create a *seller's* market by attracting hordes of buyers who compete with one another. (Of course, this is wonderful if you are a seller.)

Another way to access some of the best deals is to be the first buyer to see the unadvertised "pocket listings" from business brokers.

Lionel Haines, a writer and entrepreneur, says,

"You must act like a hunter, not a trapper."

You can't wait for opportunity to come around. You must seek it out, and when you find it you must know what to do or you will lose your chance.

Imperviousness to unhealthy buyer fever.

You don't want to catch a *fatal* dose of it. (You do want to enjoy a *healthy* dose of it!)

What can cause a *fatal* case of buyer fever?

Symptoms include:

- Buyer competition, real or phony. It can increase your temperature.

- Deciding upon your acquisition criteria after you commence your search.

- Advisory team infected by conflict-of-interest.

- Inadequate due diligence.

- Being unaware of the selling prices and terms of sale for similar businesses.

- Weak-knee negotiating.

- Too-easily influenced by the seller and seller representatives.

- Using "good luck" business valuation methods.

- Non-definitive purchase and sale agreement.

- Verbal promises, representations or understandings.

- Premature closing.

It is okay, and maybe useful, to catch buyer fever. But, as in love, it's a good idea to know what makes you hot in a good way and what does not.

"Death" from business buyer fever occurs when buyers want a particular business so badly that common sense goes out the window.

Even people who know what to do sometimes do the wrong thing, especially if they have a bad case of buyer fever.

Do you have a history of remaining unmoved and unaffected by other peoples' dangerous or worthless opinions, arguments, or suggestions? Don't let buyer fever kill you.

Business buyers who know how to search for winners don't worry about losing opportunities; worthwhile deals are like buses; more will be by soon.

Industry competence.

Competence requires experience and know-how.

Good solutions begin with attentive listening, recognition, and comprehension of the problem.

This continually assumes that the knowledge of the relevant market situation and the competitive landscape as well as the corresponding success factors is at hand. And thus - a high degree of Sector Competency.

(Thanks to Andersch, the management consulting firm.)

Industry proficiency.

It's a good idea to buy the kind of company whose industry is well-known by the acquirer.

Risk is usually greater for buyers venturing into lines of business outside their hands-on experience. Some sellers and brokers won't talk to those kinds of buyers.

Check this out, which you may not want to sign up for but you can glean useful info browsing the website, and then Googling this topic:

Deloitte: The Industry Proficiency Program is a self-paced program that you can use to help guide your industry skill-building activities and recognize your accomplishments as you achieve your goals at each industry milestone.

Integrity.

Everyone thinks they know what this means. So, I'm not going to preach to the choir. Instead, here's a snippet from online:

Honesty, by definition, is to tell the truth and being true.

Integrity is having strong moral principles based on honesty and to follow those principles religiously.

That said, honesty can also be used as synonym for integrity.

Intend to buy the right business the right way.

Some people acquire the right business the wrong way, which can turn winners into losers. And, too many people are surprised to discover they bought the wrong business.

Read Ted Leverette's other books: *How to Buy the Right Business the Right Way—Dos, Don'ts & Profit Strategies* and *How to Get ALL the Money You Want For Your Business Without Stealing It* (Choose the USA or Canadian version.)

The *Business Buyer Advocate* methodologies are more important to me than the information. (There are many business consulting and dealmaking informational books, videos, social media websites, and other resources that are readily available.) But our processes, our skills that we share with clients, and how and when we help clients when they need it. That is what differentiates us from other advisors and it empowers our clients.

Intuition.

Go with your gut feel. If your gut tells you something's wrong, it's time to get away, no matter how good a match the other factors appear to be on the surface.

Investment in how-to info.

Anyone who knows me (Ted Leverette) knows I'm critical of do-it-yourselfers. Why? Too many of them don't know what they don't know (and must know) to achieve worthwhile done deals. Consequently, their dream fades away or it turns into their living nightmare. And then they and their lawyer hope to pin the blame on someone else. (Just kidding!)

Yes, it's important to invest in your business buying education. But you'll have more questions no matter how much you think you're learning. That's the thing about reading books, Googling all night and taking courses (which I, of course want you to do by purchasing mine): You're not going to know what the experts know. So, decide: Do you want to profitably buy a company? Or do you want to learn how to be a dealmaking expert? It's one or the other, unless you have surplus years to invest (or waste).

Keep in motion pending deals.

Procrastination can drown deals. Doers beat deliberators.

Delays can kill the deal; keep the ball in motion.

Procrastination is one of the leading causes for deals falling through. The longer it takes to achieve a meeting of the minds between buyers, sellers, their advisors and sources of financing, the more likely the deal will crater. Dealmaking is like a pendulum. It must stay in motion with activity swinging back and forth between the buyer and seller. Complete stops are not smart.

What is your opportunity cost?

The longer it takes you to buy a business, the higher your opportunity cost. You forego the monthly salary and business profit you could earn from owning a company until you consummate a purchase. You waste money fast.

Example: If it takes you one more week to get started or to meet the next seller of a mature, profitable, fairly priced company, and you would earn $20,000 more per month from your target business, $5,000 is your effective loss (each week!).

A delay in buying can cost you as much as paying too much. It's like standing on the sidelines during a rising real estate or stock market.

Know or are shown how to recognize a good business.

See also: *Industry Proficiency*.

Know the product and industry.

Knowing the industry and willing to learn through conferences and seminars.

See also: *Industry Proficiency*.

Know about dealmaking.

We're referring to buy/sell transactions.

Know their rights.

Too many potential buyers of small and midsize businesses do not know what is fair and reasonable during their interaction with business sellers, business brokers, M&A intermediaries, professional service providers, sources of financing and other people and organizations they encounter during the buyers' process to locate and purchase worthwhile businesses for sale.

Uninformed potential buyers unnecessarily frustrate and complicate themselves and their relationships with the people and organizations they need the most, upon which buyers must rely to buy the right business the right way.

Read at PartnerOnCall.com: *Bill of Rights for Buyers of Small and Midsize Businesses.*

Learn how to buy a business.

Do it to avoid mistakes in the marketplace that can foreclose the buyers' opportunities.

In the buy-sell world it's important that everybody understand some basics including people will get frustrated; there will be deal fatigue; and, there are set ranges of value so just because an owner sees a $500 million firm selling for 10 times EBITDA doesn't mean a company with revenue of $5-10 million will get the same multiple.

What's the best way to learn how to buy a business? The more effort the better, right? Not so, new research shows. People who excel aren't necessarily those who study longest. Instead, they study smart—planning and actively seeking help. And the best kind of help comes from people proven to be among the leading experts.

Listen to the horse's mouth.

If you get information about something from the horse's mouth, you get it from someone who is involved in it and knows a lot about it. That's why savvy people who read my books, for example, contact me to talk about it. They want to know or verify what is critically important in the how-to material. They want to zero in on subtleties, during conversations, especially insights beyond the printed pages. You've seen this if you've attended seminars and lectures. The audience who hangs around, afterwards, wants to talk to the speaker so they can refine their understanding.

Mindset.

Definition: A set of beliefs or a way of thinking that determine somebody's behavior and outlook.

I think the business acquisition process starts with *mindset*. All the other attributes, beliefs, behaviors take place along the way. By *mindset* I mean we imagine what could be, and then when we act to make happen what we want so we can get it. But without the guts to persevere, no matter how many lousy companies we encounter, no matter how many bad deals we avoid, no matter what, we achieve our goal. We see ourselves as being in business, and then we own our company.

Having the correct mindset that you can get a deal done.

Motivation.

To achieve a done deal.

The buyer and seller have to be motivated. And usually it has to be more than one motive to compel people to do what it takes to buy or sell a company.

Negotiator.

Negotiating expertise: Have it or hire it. Or at least have the ability not to trip over one's own feet.

Not a know-it-all.

Do you want to be like this hotshot? According to a *New York Times*, August 13, 2017, article, "The Incredible Shrinking Sears," the subtitle addresses know-it-alls: "How a financial wizard took over a giant of American retailor, and presided over its epic decline." Hedge fund moneybags (not so much money anymore), Edward S. Lampert, controlling Sears "borrowed to the hilt." This genius also presided over Sears selling valuable assets and suffering cash flow pinches. Not to mention "profit, for Lampert and his investors, has not materialized." See the article for reading and weeping.

Potential buyers of companies: See this topic: *Capable Acquisition Advisory Team.*

Not dangerously impulsive.

Willie Nelson said "The second mouse gets the cheese."

Want to put a stop to hasty decisions, get the self-control boost you need? Click to read an article by Fast Company.

Oh, you're a *New York Times* kind of person? Read: "When impulsiveness turns dangerous." Excerpt: Researchers have begun to resolve the contrary nature of impulsivity, identifying the elements that distinguish benign experimentation from self-destructive acts.

See also: *Imperviousness to Unhealthy Buyer Fever.*

Numbers and timing.

Pay the price.

There might not be anything more costly than a cheap person.

Learn how to accurately value small and midsize companies. Or hire an expert. And then pay the seller what it is worth.

Don't waste your time (and everyone else's) by nickeling and diming sellers. Remember, time is money. And sellers of worthwhile companies divert their attention to more reasonable buyers.

See also: *Keeping in Motion the Pending Deal(s).*

Plan and act.

Plan the work; follow the plan.

Prepared.

Be adequately prepared.

Ready, willing and able: Ready, because self-examination, education and market research allow you to know a good business when it surfaces. Willing means the buyer has resolved fear and timing issues. Able tells me they have or know where the money is coming from to proceed.

Relationships.

People wanting to sell or buy a business screen each other to make sure it's a fit.

Focusing on the relationship means not allowing disagreements to damage the interpersonal relationship.

Resilience.

The capacity to recover quickly from difficulties; toughness.

Buying companies is like being a kid again. You get to fall down a lot, skin your knees, be bullied, ignored, and misunderstood. If you don't run home crying to mommy, buying a business could be wonderfully fun and lucrative. More so, after closing.

Resourceful.

You better be resourceful because your cup probably won't runneth over with worthwhile companies to buy (unless you have years to search and deal-make). The easiest, fastest and least expensive way (remember "opportunity costs') is to hire someone, who doesn't have a conflict-of-interest, to guide you to and through the hidden market to search for the *best* companies for sale. (I'm applying for the job!)

See also: Access the Hidden Market.

Respect.

Showing respect for the seller will win you a lot of 'goodies' vs being an ass towards the seller.

Self-confident.

Realistically so!

Self-sufficient.

But not a do-it-yourselfer!

It's good to seek the opinions of others. It may be good to seek and get the consensus of others. But be wary of decision-making by group consensus or management-by-committee. Perhaps you should give up thinking about being a business owner if your Facebook connections are going to participate.

Supportive family and friends.

One of the first lessons I learned (in the 1970s) when I created our consulting niche (*Business Buyer Advocate*®) was how to increase the probability of a done deal.

It's when I realized that my potential clients' spouse or significant other MUST attend our meetings before I was hired.

Oh yes, you should have heard the objections: "I'm too busy!" "She's too busy!" "He's too busy." To which I replied: "Too busy to avoid losing the family's life savings and to see the wannabe buyer' self-esteem tank after buying a loser?"

Lucky for me I got hired by the right kinds of people. (Whew!)

See also: *Avoiding Toxic People.*

Tenacity.

Yep!

Thorough.

During prospecting, analyzing, deal structuring, transitioning the company from the seller to the buyer, etc.

Uninformed exuberance has hurt more business buyers than lousy or overpriced acquisitions and mergers.

Trust.

If the buyer and seller don't have a fundamental level of trust between them, it's hard to do any deal.

Why?

Why do you want to own a company? Why buy one?

Buyers must, also, know why the owner wants to sell the company. Some buyers walk away from potential transactions if they don't believe or detect the seller's *real* reason for offering the company for sale.

Willing and able to assume the demands.

Including financial, mental and physical demands of buying and owning a business.

Willing to give up to get.

Willing to give up what you have to get what you want because you think you have what it takes.

Willing to learn.

About businesses, industries, economics and dealmaking.

Willing to proceed despite fear and Doubting Thomases.

Overcoming fear of failure is essential to success. Risk and failure are a part of success and they create the opportunity for learning and improving. Unreasonable fears of failure must be overcome to continue to act on one's desires to be successful. The lack of fear can be just as dangerous in leading to complacency and over-confidence.

Are you capable of resolving fear of failure?

Dr. Phil, I think, replied to people with irrational fears of failure: "And then what will happen?"

Ignore Doubting Thomases, the people who are prone to unreasonably scoff and discourage your aspirations.

I'm not referring to a Devil's Advocate who takes positions he or she does not necessarily agree with (or simply suggests an alternative position from the accepted norm or from your opinion). It can be good to do this for the sake of debate or to explore the thought further. This can be good if performed responsibly and without a hidden agenda that is illegitimately adverse to your self-interest.

What, specifically, is the financial or personal loss you fear?

Can you afford the loss? If not, and especially if you don't have the guts to try, maybe now is a good time to put to bed your fantasy about buying/owning a company.

Chapter 3

The Big Picture

Buying a business is like peeling an onion. (Yes, I know. This is an overused metaphor. Forgive me. And now, to continue: "Peeling an onion" is a vivid comparison that we can use.)

When peeling an onion, it is usually best to start at the outermost ring and then peel off one layer at a time. Especially if you suspect rot or insects inside the bulb. Of course, you could cut to the chase and slice it into quarters. But doing so wrecks its appearance if, in fact, you want the onion to retain its natural shape for whatever use you want to put it.

If you want to retain the original shape as much as possible, first you peel off the papery layers. And then you remove and discard the skin. And then you can continue to peel off one layer at a time. Keep this in mind if you want to keep in motion your pending merger or acquisition throughout the entire process of preparing and then buying or merging a small or midsize company.

It's a good way to delve into and progress through the phases of business buying or merging. Do it one layer at a time, so you can thoroughly understand what's happening. Slow down to go fast. Narrow your focus. Detect the company's opportunities and vulnerabilities.

Proceeding sequentially layer-by-layer increases the probability that you will see what you need to see. That why, working as a

Business Buyer Advocate ®, I and my clients use my proprietary *Street-Smart 22-Step Acquisition Sequence* ™. It integrates these phases essential to buyers: searching for (and finding) businesses that buyers cannot find (on their own) on the hidden market of sellers, due diligence, creative financing, pricing businesses for sale, dealmaking, post-acquisition due diligence and transition management.

The most successful buyers, before they search, prepare themselves to efficiently find worthwhile companies (the more the merrier) so they achieve profitable done deals. This book begins by showing you how to prepare *yourself* and then it explains how to *find* the *right* acquisition or merger.

Here is the big picture: Before you concern yourself with businesses for sale, begin by detecting and evaluating *your* opportunities and vulnerabilities; what *you* bring to the table and *what else* you need so you can achieve the best deal, at the lowest cost and in the least amount of time.

Prepare Yourself

Preparation begins with evaluation. Of yourself. Your advisory team can help you perceive reality.

Your self-assessment, and what you do to improve capabilities, determines to what degree the marketplace of sellers, sources of financing and others will perceive you to be qualified to buy a business.

What's your penalty for not being properly prepared to search for a business?

- You appear foolish if you make a bad first impression on sellers and their advisors.

- If your ineptitude taints your list of target businesses, what will remain to buy?

- Instead of having, within days or weeks, businesses that meet your criteria, with little or no buyer competition, expect it to take months (or never) to discover a deal worth doing.

The Qualified Buyer

- Credentials are suitable for the target business(s);

- capable business acquisition advisory team;

- financial resources are sufficient for your target kind of deal;

- reasonable acquisition criteria for target business is compatible with above;

- and you are motivated to achieve a done deal—ASAP!

Search for Opportunities

This is where you put to work what you learned and acquired during preparation. It's about implementation, not planning. Proceed sequentially through these four phases.

Phase 1

Acquisition criteria. The more requirements and variables you defined (during preparation), the less time you'll waste during search.

Advisory team. Deploy people with a proven history of working for buyers and sellers of the kind and size of deal you intend. They have facilitated deals that should and did occur. They are dealmakers, deal closers.

Capability statement. Show your credentials, of course. And your financial capability to do the size and kind of deal you intend.

Phase 2

Elements of negotiation. You and your advisory team, while you were preparing yourself, can better-serve your self-interest if you deploy the kinds of negotiating techniques that are proven to work well for the kind and size of deal you intend. It is not a good idea to deploy generic negotiating techniques.

Interview technique. Communicating with brokers, sellers and their advisors is not like interviewing for a job. While you were preparing was the best time to nail down the best ways to interview people (and be interviewed).

Search strategy. There are lots of ways to find opportunities, some much better than others. Deploy the tactics you identified while you were preparing yourself.

Phase 3

Contact acquisition targets. Use the tools you acquired while you were preparing.

Phase 4

Screen sellers and potential partners. Use the timing and scripts you created during preparation.

Letter of intent. Refer to the various kinds of documents you acquired during preparation.

Okay, that is the big picture. The rest of this book delves into the elements of preparation and search. You'll read facts, tips, dos, don'ts and profit strategies in use by the most successful dealmakers and advisors.

Chapter 4

Know What You Are Up Against

You can't BUY the right business if you can't FIND it!

The first step is to know what you are up against. And then you can mitigate the risks and exploit the opportunities. You can make your and everyone else's jobs easier while you are interacting with people and organizations on your way to buying the right business the right way. You can encourage an environment of collaboration instead of confrontation.

This chapter details what is happening and what to do about it.

Are you a disgruntled business buyer?

Some people are surprised to discover they bought the wrong business. And some people acquire the *right* business the *wrong* way, which turned a winner into a loser.

The good news (sort of) is a disaster might be recoverable.

Whatever you call it (calamity, catastrophe, debacle, disaster, failure, fiasco, mess, misadventure, pitfall, tragedy) it's not what you expected.

Surviving does not necessarily mean getting out, uninjured, of the mess. You might survive but the wounds might be costly. What you read in this book can help you avoid business buying mistakes and help you fix or alleviate problems.

You can avoid, or detect after closing, the most common business buying mistakes. Our suggestions can help you see beyond the obvious when you dig deeper into your mess. The topic below can help people navigate through the business buying minefield.

Mistakes made during the process of buying a business.

An ounce of prevention is worth a pound of cure. That's the theme for this topic if you have not already bought a business. If you have, with regrets, bought a company, keep reading for ideas to increase the efficiency and profitability of any company.

Buyer Fever (the most common mistake).

You need to be hot for a business, but it can kill you if you get too hot too soon and for the wrong reasons. You'll know when you have the fever. It's when you cross the threshold of being a calculating person to thinking you must have this business; let's get this deal done. It's okay to be excited. If you're not, you're probably examining the wrong business.

But buyer enthusiasm isn't enough. It can lead to a fatal case of buyer fever. We tell buyers to be careful if they act on what they think they know, because they can make big mistakes if they are wrong or don't know everything they should know about purchasing a business.

"Death" from business buyer fever occurs when a buyer wants a particular business so badly that common sense goes out the window. Even people who know what to do sometimes do the wrong thing, especially if they have a bad case of buyer fever.

Believing "I'll know it when I see it" causes sellers and brokers to view you as being unprepared. The window-shopping search tactic encourages buyer's fever.

Many mistakes buyers make are errors of omission, not knowing what to do. Even people who know what to do sometimes do the wrong thing, especially if they have a bad case of buyer fever – wanting a particular business so badly they suspend their common sense.

What can cause a fatal case of buyer fever?

Symptoms include:

- Buyer competition, real or phony. It can increase your temperature.

- Deciding upon your acquisition criteria after you commence your search.

- Advisory team infected by conflict-of-interest.

- Inadequate due diligence.

- Being unaware of the selling prices and terms of sale for similar businesses.

- Weak-kneed negotiating. Too-easily influenced by the seller and seller representatives.

- Using "good luck" business valuation techniques.

- Non-definitive purchase and sale agreement. Verbal representations or understandings.

- Premature closing.

Business buyers who know how to search for winners don't worry about losing acquisition opportunities; worthwhile deals are like buses; more will be by soon.

Absentee owner.

"I'm an absentee owner!" is easier said than successfully done. Ask your advisors and business owners about this. Despite what the seller told you, is it necessary for you to work fulltime? Is that okay with you?

If the seller claimed to be an "absentee owner," what was the reason for selling? After all, the seller didn't have to be there to make money, right? Did / does a fulltime manager run the company?

Where does the buck stop with absentee ownership? To what degree are performance measurement and reporting procedures in place? What about, you, the buyer who wants to be an absentee owner? Do you want your investment, profit and risk in someone else's hands? What if your manager (or another key employee) realizes s/he doesn't need you? And quits the company to start a competing business? When the cat's away the mice will play.

Beware of Traps and Risks of NDAs and PGs

How much are you aware of these two traps and risks for buyers AND sellers of businesses? The first begins with the Non-Disclosure Agreement (NDA) and the second arises later regarding the Personal Guarantee (PG).

- These topics are further covered in my book: *How to Buy the Right Business the Right Way.*

Spoiler alert:

- Naive searchers/buyers sign NDAs and PGs foisted on them.

- Unreasonable demands by sellers repel the savviest and perhaps the best-qualified buyers.

They do it because they don't know what they don't know. They simply (and mistakenly) believe they're supposed to do it.

Both of these legal documents are negotiable if you know how to do it.

Acquisition advisory team was inadequate.

The typical process for finding a worthwhile acquisition and then achieving a profitable done deal consists of evaluating and preparing the buyer, searching for businesses that match the buyer's criteria, due diligence, financing, valuing/pricing the company and dealmaking. If any of the specialists on the team have a conflict-of-interest or don't know enough, the buyer will be left holding the bag or, perhaps, waste professional fees and not achieve a done deal.

Here's insight provided by a dealmaker:

"The most important thing is not to buy a business that is not an appropriate fit or where you don't know about all the "skeletons in the closet." I work with my buy-side clients to make sure that we are looking at businesses that meet their criteria and that a thorough due diligence process is completed. There is no such thing as a perfect business, every business has warts; you just need to make sure that the warts are not malignant. That being said, most problems can be fixed, with a good plan of action by a good business person. Specifically, a written plan for 30 days, 90 days and one year. Make decisions, especially the hard ones, quickly and don't look back."

Acquisition criteria was faulty.

The most common assertion we hear from naïve wannabe buyers is "I'll know it when I see it!" We think (and sometimes say) "Yeah, sure, you betcha!" Defining what you bring to the table and what you seek are the first steps. They include your resources, search criteria for screening sellers, benchmarks (sales and profit trends, industry performance stats), business evaluation standards and the probable range of *asking* prices for the target companies. If you upfront establish realistic acquisition criteria, it does not take long to discover winners for sale, especially if you shop on the hidden market of businesses quietly for sale by-owner.

Buyer competition fuels dumb deals.

The best business brokers create buyer competition, which encourages a bidding war. Baby Boomers hunting for acquisitions are increasing buyer competition. Financial reporters say the greatest transfer of wealth has been and will continue to occur over the next decade; much of it is tied up in family-businesses. Too many buyers do dumb deals because they have to outbid the horde of other buyers. You can avoid most of the competing buyers by accessing the hidden market of mature, profitable and fairly priced small and mid-size companies that are quietly for sale by-owner. According to one of the most prolific dealmakers, *Arnold S. Goldstein*, whose tell-it-like-it-is books and educational materials have guided people for decades: "Most sellers turn to brokers after all other efforts to sell have failed." *Your* competitive advantage dissolves once a broker is on scene.

Buyer is unqualified to fix or manage the company.

Too many buyers, whose pending deal looked good on paper, are shocked to discover, after buying the company, that they have a tiger by the tail; that they don't have enough business IQ to avoid being mauled. If this is your situation, immediately hire professional advisors. Don't think so? Good luck.

Buyer didn't follow optimum acquisition sequence.

You might have jumped the gun, resulting in a post-closing mess, if you did not sensibly progress through all the steps to find and buy a business. Our proprietary *Street-Smart 22-Step Acquisition Sequence* ™ differentiates *Business Buyer Advocates* ® from typical professional service providers. Our methodologies can avoid pitfalls and keep buyers on track.

Buyer's cash reserve insufficient.

Note the word, "buyer's." This means you. Rarely do small and midsize businesses have sufficient cash, positive cash flow or borrowing power to seize the opportunities and to fix the problems that arise shortly after the company changes hands. It won't be good if you cannot dip into your own pocket for funding.

Buyer's search activity insufficient.

The dearth of mature, profitable and fairly-priced small and midsize businesses during and after the Great Recession is throttling dealmaking. There has been as much as an 80% decline of worthwhile sellers the past few years.

It's easier and more productive to use a shotgun than a rifle. Too many wannabe buyers have too few targets to hit. The following stats are from a study we did. Your experience may differ. These figures can differ during recessions. And the type and size of business affects these statistics.

Easily vulnerable to theft or embezzlement.

Experts report that company employees steal and embezzle more than outsiders. Pre-employment screening is the first line of defense. Policies, procedures, control, surveillance, fidelity bonds, reporting and supervision can keep a tight rein on assets, intellectual property, purchasing and anything else you don't want to lose.

Think twice before knowingly purchasing the kind of business where theft or embezzlement is prevalent. Avoid this risk is while searching for worthwhile acquisitions.

Easy entry by startups into the industry.

The sub-headline of a Forbes article, touting the next wave of business startups should be a warning call instead of an invitation to would-be entrepreneurs: "Food, booze, and cost-saving firms top IBISWorld list of industries with low barriers to entry and high growth potential." If you bought into this kind of situation, saturation by competitors is likely to thwart or kill your business.

Emotions getting in the way.

Here's insight provided from a dealmaker:

"People make physical mistakes. Basketball players miss layups and dunks, we hit our thumb when pounding a nail (ouch!), football players drop catches right in their hands and business people don't get the right words out to convey value and therefore lose the customer. Especially in sports, I can understand this. One of the best lessons for business is to follow your plan; don't get too excited and don't get too down. Just do your job the way you're supposed to do without getting caught up in the moment."

— *John Martinka, Business Buyer Advocate* ®

Insulting people won't attract or engage sellers.

Too many wannabe buyers insult sellers and their representatives; this can end the possibility of a worthwhile done deal. The most attractive sellers dump buyers that are impolite, excessively demanding or don't efficiently handle due diligence and the buying process. These behaviors motivate some sellers to "bad-mouth" the buyer among the seller's friendly competitors. Similarly, brokers might warn their friendly competitors about nuisance buyers.

Limited vision before or after acquisition.

Business buyers who closed deals shortly before the Great Recession, and did not anticipate it coming, got a big surprise. Valuing the business is not enough, especially relying too much on the historical performance. Evaluate the industry (of the business and its customers, suppliers and sources of financing, landlord) plus the economy before and after closing. Don't be caught flatfooted.

Poor positioning of the buyer during search.

Typical buyers do not cast a wide enough search net. So, they decrease their odds of buying a company, and it takes longer to achieve a done deal, because they have so few choices.

Settling for whatever your search discovers.

Too many buyers settle for whatever they can find because they cannot find something better. Here's why:

Not searching where the best deals are found. Buyers forego some of the best opportunities if they do not adequately access the hidden market of sellers. It's where you can avoid buyer competition because these businesses are not visible to the general public. It's where up to 80% of the mature, profitable and fairly priced small and midsize companies are quietly for sale by-owner. Few of these owners advertise their business for sale. Some of these winners are not yet on the market, but they and other sellers want to meet buyers. But few of these owners will admit they are for sale to buyers they don't know because they don't want the word to get out that they are for sale or they don't want to expose their offering to unqualified buyers.

Private-party buyers lack credibility. Even if a buyer can do everything a professional advisor does to contact potential sellers, one essential ingredient is missing: Third-party communication and credibility by an acquisition intermediary.

Mysterious identity. An owner, rightfully so, is suspicious of people who inquire about a business being for sale, particularly a private party unknown to the company manager or owner. Acquisition advisors make it their business to be known within the business community, by owners—and their advisors, such as attorneys, accountants, bankers.

Inconsistent search effort. "The best laid plans of men . . ." You know how it goes. Making a commitment is not the same as achieving a commitment. Think about your history of best intentions. Health, family, job, sports, lifestyle? Most people who say they will own a company never do. Most give up because they can't find enough winners (for sale) on reasonable terms.

Distaste for rejection. Nobody likes rejection. It's easier to take, however, if you're paid for it. A *Business Buyer Advocate's* job is to take the brunt of rejection, several times a day, from owners who don't want to talk to you. When we search for you, you are fresh to see the best of what's available. This is important. How much do you enjoy rejection? Will you enjoy the constant follow up necessary to get through to an owner?

<u>You have a life!</u> I don't think I've ever met someone who wasn't already busy. Most people complain that they don't have enough time. Do you have enough time to conduct a search, during the narrow range of business hours when the owner is present? Our business is making contacts for you. The rest of our life doesn't infringe on our intention to find you a good company.

Unfunded and contingent liabilities mean cash crunches.

Accrued vacation and other accrued paid time off can be a hidden liability in businesses. What is the value of it? Must it be paid in cash to terminating employees? Who will do the work, at what additional cost, when employees consume their benefit? What about underfunded or unfunded pension plans, warranties and service contracts? Screen for these things early in your review of companies for sale.

Unrealistic or uninformed expectations.

Depending upon the source of this observation, it's said that up to 95% of wannabe buyers don't buy a business. The sad truth is some of these buyers waste a considerable amount of money during their failed attempts to find and purchase a company. Some of them deplete too much of their life savings, which means they cannot afford to acquire a company. Wasting money on deals that fall through adversely affects the buyers' financial security. You can avoid these unfortunate outcomes if, before you begin hunting for sellers, you thoroughly research the industries in which your target companies do business. See publicly available industry ratios, which will assist you in benchmarking a target company's financial performance against industry norms. According to the *Institute of Business Appraisers*, the best proof of the value of a business is the sale price. Numerous (and credible) sources of buy/sell stats are available; besides reporting selling prices the best databases reveal the key terms of the buy/sell transaction. One of these information providers compiles and reports information on up to 88 data points highlighting the financial and transactional details of the sales of privately and closely held companies. Buyers lacking such insight are hobbled by their unrealistic expectations.

Warren Buffett on searches.

When a media pundit asked one of the richest investors in the world about his firm's (Berkshire Hathaway Inc.) huge cash position, which exists because there are too few worthy potential business acquisitions, Buffet replied: "It's a painful position to be in – but not as painful as doing something stupid." The dilemma so far hasn't prevented Buffet from increasing the firm's value during the past four decades.

Working capital risk leads to insolvency.

One of the first facts that street-smart buyers uncover, early in their screening of companies for sale, is how much working capital is necessary. It takes more working capital if inventory is too low or if there is or will be insufficient borrowing power in the company they might acquire. Undercapitalization can put you out of business faster than operating losses.

Buyers suffer because they ignore this truism:

You can pay too much for a good business, but you can't pay too little for a lousy one. The problems we feature in this book stem from defective acquisition techniques, not a lack of good businesses. Every year, thousands of business buyers buy the right business the right way. But other buyers wish that they had not purchased a business, because they bought the wrong business or the right business the wrong way.

Be suspicious of "Seller's Discretionary Earnings."

What kinds of "earnings"?

Should it be pretax or after tax? What kinds of taxes?

Does the owner's and/or the company's income tax returns portray the profitability?

What about these commonly expressed representations of "benefit"?

- Adjusted net cash flow

- Discretionary cash flow

- Seller's discretionary earnings

- Seller's discretionary cash flow

- Owner's discretionary earnings

- Owner's discretionary cash flow

- Company annual adjusted net cash flow

All those phrases can be misleading. Very.

Did you notice the changing point of view in those titles? From "seller" to "owner" to "company"?

Now is a good time for you (i.e., the business buyer) to think about what will be the company's actual net cash flow, and the actual net profit, after you acquire the company.

You can get more insight into this topic in my book: *How to **Buy** the Right Business the Right Way*.

Alarming article by Business Brokerage Press.

Business Brokerage Press makes an alarming statement that deserves a response from the other side of the dealmaking table.

Their article showcases an avoidable mistake made by too many business brokers, buyers and sellers. And, despite warnings from dealmaking experts, the self-defeating behavior continues.

It usually happens within the first few hours of unsuspecting buyers setting out to find sellers of small or midsize companies.

Who needs to know about this? Anyone advising or hoping to sell a small or midsize company or buy the right business the right way.

Sources of financing cannot fund deals if this mistake stops deals from occurring.

I'm referring to this article by *Business Brokerage Press*: "Are You Shaking Hands or Hitting Send?"

In my opinion, as a *Business Buyer Advocate*, this candid article, written for a largely business brokerage audience, raises a touchy topic that can either make or break a business buyer's opportunity to achieve a worthwhile done deal.

Buyers and their advisors are risking too much if they don't find and read the article and heed the street-smart advice you can read in my books. Doing so enables you to materially increase the probability that you (or people you represent) will buy the *right* business the *right* way.

And, if you're a business broker, you can sell more businesses more quickly.

Advisors can help clients achieve done deals if their clients deploy the tactics I explain.

Okay, let's start with four points in the article. And then I'll explain my concern and suggest ways for everyone to keep open their doors for opportunity.

1. Buyers (the real ones) are critical to the success of a business brokerage firm.

2. The potential buyer emails the broker who then, in most cases, emails the prospect an agreement of confidentiality or similar form. When that is returned, more information is supplied. From there, most firms attempt to set up an appointment. What's missing? Up to this point in the process, there is still no personal contact!

3. If a buyer's only contact with a broker is "electronic" the chances are high that the relationship will end as soon as the buyer's interest in that particular listing ends.

4. It is probably harder than ever to get buyers into your office.

You probably recognize the underlying theme for all those points: Failure to achieve worthwhile and sustainable relationships.

So, what prevents so many brokers and buyers from getting what they want?

• Brokers want people to buy the companies they've listed for sale.

• Buyers want to purchase a business.

Let's think about it.

Here's what I hear from potential business buyers; it's also what most brokers don't want to hear:

"Can you help me buy a business or show me businesses for sale?"

And then the communication does a face plant. When I, or a broker, ask: "What do you have in mind?" The buyer responds, "Oh, I don't know. I'm open-minded. I want to see what's available and then I'll decide what I might want to pursue."

Fact check: The most successful brokers won't put up with this, and they shouldn't!

Listen up, buyers: Show up with reasonable acquisition criteria. Express it in the fewest words! And then let the game begin.

"I don't know what kind of business I want, but I want to make at least xxx thousand dollars a year." Saying something like that to brokers can end the game before buyers have a chance to enter the dealmaking playing field. Why?

Brokers know that nearly everything they show to that kind of buyer is going to get the response: "No, I don't like that one; show me something else."

So, brokers ask: "Like what?"

"Oh, I won't know it until I see it!" That kind of statement is not only a foul ball; it is a game-ender.

Time is money!

Keep in mind that sellers, brokers, advisors, lenders and other gatekeepers are all busy. They want to determine whether they can make money from you. They don't have time to waste. All they want to know from you is if they can sell something to you.

They can't sell something to you if you're not prepared, ready, willing and able to buy it.

As for talking (using your voice) to sellers, brokers and other gatekeepers, especially the first time you talk to them, you must get it right. It's not simply what you say; it's how you say it.

Think about dancing. Does it feel good on the dancefloor moving around without having practiced what looks good? It's no fun embarrassing yourself on the dance floor, is it? It's no fun, and a fast way to lose your partner, if you don't know how to dance with sellers, brokers and other gatekeepers.

One of the most important things I do with clients is to help them prepare and work from scripts. And we rehearse them before my clients talk to people.

The bottom line if you're a buyer: If you want sellers, brokers and gatekeepers to keep talking to you, you must look good to them. Upfront. The first impression!

And what about talking? I mean using your voice instead of emailing or texting.

Sellers, brokers, advisors, lenders and other gatekeepers care about how they spend their time. They also care about their risk. In other words, do they see risk in a particular buyer?

They don't want to know potential buyers who don't have what it takes to achieve a done deal.

They also don't want to deal with buyers who make everyone crazy on the way to a done deal.

Brokers, sellers and advisors don't want to work with buyers who might blow themselves up, for they tend to drag down other people with them.

Buyers erode opportunity if they are an unprepared rookie or they seem to be a red flag.

Let's think about being a rookie. Even the richest and most successful people, even people who've handled mega mergers or acquisitions . . . they don't know enough about buying a small or midsize business. People on the other side of the dealmaking table know this; brokers and sellers will cope with rookies, to a limited extent.

As for red flags, if you raise them, the other side shoots them down. The best way to soften your "rookiness" is to showcase, upfront, the quality of your team of dealmaking advisors.

I don't think I've ever met an honest seller, broker or advisor wanting to work with DIYers. Sure, some of them do it; and then they abort those DIYers whenever a more-prepared prospect shows up. It's why you read posts by buyers complaining online about sellers who dumped them to sell the company to someone else.

And one more tip: Whoever says it in fewest words wins ™.

I am not implying that buyers don't disclose what should be disclosed. I'm telling you that you make better impressions when you say it in fewest words.

In fact, the more that a buyer blathers, the more likely s/he is to raise red flags. Red flags disturb listeners. Keep it short and sweet!

People who say more than necessary are, sometimes, the kinds of people who ask every question in the book, questions many of which are totally inappropriate for whatever they're doing.

That tips off the other side that they might be coping with someone with a deadly condition for dealmaking: analysis-to-paralysis.

Tip for buyers:

Reasonably disclose information about yourself and your plans. But you may not get to second base if you don't know how to ask the right questions the right way at the right time.

Too many buyers lose their opportunity because they don't know how to get the other side of their dealmaking table to disclose what the buyer wants to know.

Question improperly; drive away opportunity.

Okay, so what if you're a rookie?

Can you say what needs to be said in fewest words, showing us your strong suit? And will you do your homework? And seek expert advice? And then follow direction from people known to facilitate deals that should occur?

Right now, let's recognize an important fact of life. My guess is that 99% of people thinking about buying a small or midsize company begin by visiting websites that advertise businesses for sale. Such as bizbuysell.com.

And then their bullshit meter red lines. They're turned off by the promotional advertising.

But . . . that doesn't drive buyers away from websites such as bizbuysell.com. Why not?

Here's why: Most buyers, nowadays, are reluctant to pick up their phone and dial business brokers. It's simply too easy to see online what appears to be the entire marketplace of businesses for sale.

(Of course, those of us in the dealmaking industries know that what can be discovered for sale online is, arguably, less than half of what's actually for sale.)

But, let's not think about that right now.

Let's continue with what's actually happening in the marketplace.

So, buyers browse the listings on websites such as bizbuysell. com. And then, well, let's go back to the text from the article that has caused me to write about this topic:

- The potential buyer emails the broker who then, in most cases, emails the prospect an agreement of confidentiality or similar form. When that is returned, more information is supplied. From there, most firms attempt to set up an appointment. What's missing? Up to this point in the process, there is still no personal contact!

- If a buyer's only contact with a broker is "electronic" the chances are high that the relationship will end as soon as the buyer's interest in that particular listing ends.

Yep, it's true: The relationship will end as soon as the buyer's interest in that particular listing ends.

Okay, brokers and buyers, here's what will work:

Buyers telephone brokers.

Buyers say: "I'm looking for these specific kinds of businesses that have these specific kinds of features." (The more descriptive the better.) "I have sufficient cash for the down payment to purchase a company priced between X and Y dollars. And I have more cash for working capital, if necessary, to inject into the company after closing. I want to buy a business with a proven profit history that qualifies for business acquisition financing with an SBA-guarantee."

It's also important to tell brokers the kinds of businesses that do not interest you.

Can you see how that kind of talk shows brokers you're a good prospect? Sellers, too, like buyers with definitive acquisition criteria.

Brokers (and advisors and sellers) like to hear that you've done your homework about business buying; that you won't waste their time; that you're not a perpetual tire kicker; you're a doer not a dreamer, not a ditherer.

What should buyers disclose upfront to brokers?

Being transparent is really important. It's not enough to honestly tell brokers and sellers what you want. You must also, upfront, favorably impress them with what you bring to the table. Such as your capability to buy and then successfully manage the kind and size of business you want to buy.

Said another way: Sellers, brokers, advisors and others are nervous when buyers are not reasonably transparent. People who can help buyers get into business don't want to wonder whether a buyer could be more trouble than s/he is worth.

Buyers are like buses; more will come along soon. So, savvy people on the dealmaking playing field avoid people exhibiting certain kinds of behavior.

Buyers want sellers and brokers thinking: I think I can sell this prospect something.

This is what motivates people to keep talking, to tell you what they think you need to know.

The best brokers and the savviest sellers know how to keep the information flowing to worthwhile buyers.

Buyers don't have to beg while trying to get the attention brokers. Buyers who want brokers (and anyone else) to pay attention and respond must make it worthwhile. Me, me, me doesn't work.

Us, us, us can attract people to each other who stand to benefit from each other.

(Remember what I said earlier: 24/7 brokers are being contacted by wannabe buyers; buyers are like buses. Brokers get on buses that take them where they and their sellers want to go. When brokers doubt buyers, they ignore them.)

Buyers must have their ducks in a row before communicating with anyone who is necessary to achieve a worthwhile done deal. Show that you are targeted; that you're on a mission to achieve a done deal, the sooner the better.

And during communications, be reasonably agreeable, trying collaboration instead of confrontation.

And that idea brings us to complaints about brokers by buyers.

"The broker isn't doing enough to educate me about business buying or to counsel me during dealmaking. The broker's just trying to sell the business to me!"

This is a complaint? Sure. And it's a dumb one. Buyers inflict this problem on themselves.

Fact of life: Few brokers want to be the buyer's consultant; they want to sell their listings to buyers. The more brokers, while presenting their listings to buyers, step into the buyer's world with advice, the higher the broker's risk.

Brokers never forget that they can be target-number-one when buyers are looking for someone to blame after purchasing the right or the wrong company.

You do know, don't you, that the seller is long-gone, sipping tropical drinks in a sunny locale. Good luck finding them. And, even if you do, the seller has the buyer's money to fend off buyer's remorse . . . and anyone else trying to pass the buck to the former owner.

Sensible buyers hire advisors whose loyalty is only to the buyer.

Ask your team when to invoke their name(s) when talking to brokers and sellers. It's important for the other side to know that you have proven dealmakers on call, not deal killers. Introducing your team in the wrong way or too soon repels brokers and sellers. Deferring it too long can cause people to think you might be an unprepared DIYer.

Here's a tip for buyers: Google to find examples of the listing agreements in use between brokers and sellers. Pay attention to who is obligated to do what.

Another tip for buyers: Assemble your team, or at least hire me, before you venture into the dealmaking marketplace.

You only have one chance to make a favorable impression.

Blow it with sellers and their advisors, and then you blow away your opportunity.

Don't expect people who rejected your amateur approach to welcome you back when you are newly improved. Well, there is one exception: Sellers looking for a greater fool to take off their hands their loser company; those sellers will talk to anyone.

My Seattle colleague, John Martinka, says: "No matter what the circumstances, the best way for brokers and sellers to make a sale and for buyers to buy is to get belly-to-belly. Meeting people one-on-one is the best way to communicate and get the results you want."

"It's not just business brokers and buyers who take the easy way out. Every industry is affected."

John Martinka says, "I'm not sure if it's bad training, fascination with technology, laziness, a combination or something else."

You should know my opinion about Business Brokerage Press.

Yes, it is a self-serving communicator of how-to information to its, primarily, audience of business brokers and people who serve brokers and sellers.

It's where I have been going, nearly my entire career, to continuingly expand what I know about dealmaking.

Buyers, as long as they have advisors whose only loyalty is to the buy-side of buy/sell transactions, can benefit from brokers who deploy best practices recommended by Business Brokerage Press.

The playing field, players, coaches, owners & competitors.

Chances are you are reading this book because you have been dreaming about owning a company; running it, not merely investing in it. You can probably imagine what your life will be like as a business owner. But now it is time to change the channel.

Before you start or before you delve deeper into preparing yourself to buy a business, realize that your first step is to know what to expect from the other side of the dealmaking table. You are going up against owners who want to sell their company; you will have to cope with professionals representing sellers, such as business brokers, other kinds of intermediaries and various advisors to sellers. So, before mapping out your route to sellers, it is a good idea to know the other side's strategies and tactics, and how you will counter them.

You've probably seen the multitude of websites advertising businesses for sale. Chances are you've communicated with business brokers. You might even have talked to a few sellers. If so, you are seeing some of the ways they try to influence you, control you and otherwise position themselves for their self-interest.

When you know what to expect and the motivations behind what you will face, you are better-positioned to level the dealmaking playing field, and maybe tilt it in your favor.

Let's take a look at what you should know before you go shopping.

Sellers and brokers are out to sell you a company. They want to make the most money possible. Of course, you want to buy the right business the right way for the best price. To achieve your goal, you must avoid being sweet-talked into a deal you should avoid. This chapter shows you some of the playbook in use by the "other side." Knowing what they want and how they plan to get it from you can help you avoid costly pitfalls.

Beware of these pitches from sellers and brokers.

In the old days, every Sunday, instead of reading the funnies I read the classified ads.

Now I search the Internet.

The most entertaining ads are business opportunities and businesses for sale. It's my job—really. I'm hoping to find a diamond in the rough or a true business opportunity. You see, since 1974 my firm's tagline has been: "We're the firm that investigates all the others." Business buyers and lenders hire us to help them weed out the losers and not over-pay or over-lend on the winners.

Hollywood would be proud?

Screenwriters are creative. So are advertising copywriters. But the award for "encouraging" language—with the goal to exchange your money for someone else's business — should go to business sellers.

The definition of "chutzpah" is when you murder your parents, and then plead for clemency because you're an orphan. Some sellers have chutzpah, don't they?

If you've been looking for a business to buy, you agree with me, don't you?

If you have the urge to own a business, particularly if you are getting started, my translation of common terms in advertising may cause you to chuckle and may very well save your ass-ets.

How many ways are possible to camouflage a lousy business?

"Multi-billion dollar industry" translates into field saturated with competitors.

"Must sell" is another way of saying: Looking for a greater fool.

"Call to see if you qualify." Hi, sold to *you*!

"Earn huge income immediately." Believe in the tooth fairy.

"Serious buyers only" means don't call if you expect answers to tough questions. As if they want to turn away prospects some copywriters use reverse psychology to entice you to call.

"Excellent history" suggests trouble around the corner.

"Well maintained" or **"great lifestyle"** is another way of saying unprofitable.

"Make your own hours" is work like a slave or starve.

"Excellent opportunity" is a nice way to say assume our mess.

"Dream business" is a nightmare.

"Easy" means you and everyone else the promoter can convince will compete with each other.

"Illness forces sale" could be we're sick of this lousy business—that's why we don't hire a manager to run it and send us the profit.

"Owner moving, anxious to sell" means about to go out of business.

"Call for details" equals call for sales pitch.

"Divorce forces sale" will sound familiar when *your* spouse threatens to divorce you for buying the turkey.

"Absentee owner" raises the question: If the owner doesn't need to be there to make money, why is he selling?

Franchisors selling *retail* concepts merrily proclaim, **"Premium locations!"** What they don't admit — but not good enough for us to invest *our* money.

"Priced to sell" usually means not worth owning.

"Owner makes $150K, employs wife and kids" is better than "work is our only activity, business can't afford to employ others."

"Anxious to sell" hints that you will be, too.

"Tavern: Fun lifestyle" by an owner who is tired of being robbed, smelling beer breath and coping with thieving bartenders.

"As-is condition" invites the fool born today.

"Will adjust inventory to meet buyer's ability to pay" let's you get control with insufficient inventory.

"Turnkey business" might convey we can't wait to lock the door behind us.

"Earn $900 per day, all for $9,999" When you wake up, be sure to buy another get-rich-quick opportunity so you recoup your investment. Keep doing this until you assemble a business opportunity empire, which means you have learned enough to sell one you dream up.

"Mature Company" has seen its best days.

"Executive talent for turnaround" means street-smart investors turn around and flee.

"Built-in clientele" should say we've got all the customers there are to get.

"Huge value" = worthless.

"Will pay for itself in one season" should come with its own warning label: "If not, you'll lose money for the next nine months; have lots of savings so you get a second chance."

"Established business with living quarters" so you can work 24 hours a day, seven days a week.

"Distributors wanted" suggests the territory too risky for us to staff.

"Low rent" surely means terrible location.

"Growing population" sounds better than we're still not making any money.

"Liquidating all assets" at exorbitant prices the pros won't pay.

"Major shopping center location" becomes landlord will lease to your competitors.

"Strong bonds to community." Better have a good, long term lease because the business is not relocatable.

"Free long-term support" promises that the seller will treat you like @$#&! so you don't call again.

"Owner financing" means the deal is too dumb for a bank or other source of capital to finance.

"Astounding income potential!" You'll definitely be surprised if you fall for it.

"Low down payment" almost always means the owner is thinking of shutting down but prefers to attract an unsuspecting buyer who will make payments until he, too, sees the writing on the wall.

"Part-time!" Don't give up your day job if you invest in a "part-time" opportunity.

"Free video." This is as good as it gets. Rent a movie, instead.

"Real estate included" means you don't collect rent when your business can't pay it.

"Fun business." Ask: If it's so much fun, why are you selling? Maybe I'd prefer that kind of fun, too.

"If you have the dedication to succeed." Teaser ends up being, "nobody here can turnaround this loser; maybe you can."

"50% profit" sounds good until you remember the best firms don't earn anywhere near this.

"Rated #1." Thanks, mom.

"One of a kind." You can say that, again.

"Relieve stress." Whose?

"Tired of corporate politics?" It's your turn to try to manage our band of incompetent, demanding employees.

"No selling." Turn iron into gold.

"Tired of the 9-5 grind?" Imagine working until dawn.

"Member BBB." Did we mention how often we change our company name?

"Franchise!" Nice place to send your profit. It's like renting a job. (There *are* worthwhile franchises; find one of them.)

"Principals only." We don't want to talk to your knowledgeable professional advisors, only whoever can write us a check.

"Realistic top dollar income potential." Putting "realistic" and "potential" into the same sentence is like putting a cat and dog together in a dark closet.

"Short hours" means there is not much demand for the company's product.

"Millionaire's secret!" Run ads, sell pamphlet containing secret: Run ads, sell pamphlet…

"You won't believe this until you see it," means you will not believe this when you see it.

"Riches from MLM." How to lose all your friends and cause your significant other to sleep in the other room.

"Surround yourself with beautiful women, earn thousands." Okay, I admit it. I'm curious.

Whew!

Do you think I made up these advertising headlines? I wish I were creative enough to dream up this fiction. I wouldn't be a business consultant; I would be writing bestselling novels on my laptop computer from my beach chair.

The only message sellers need to convey to attract buyers is:
"Profitable. Fair price. Will train new owner."

What about dealmaking during uncertain times?

What should you know about dealmaking during uncertain times, such as another recession? Or perhaps within a rapidly evolving industry?

Learn how to buy the right business the right way.

Don't buy a loser.

Assemble a business acquisition advisory team that does not have any conflicts-of-interest. The members should have a proven history, working for *buyers*, of *facilitating* deals that *should* occur.

Marketplace realities.

Up to 80% of businesses which sell are sold by-owner . . . depending upon the industry, size of business, its profitability and its reason for sale.

Sellers that hire the right business transfer intermediary and/ or other professional advisor usually sell their companies for higher prices on better terms than, arguably, is achieved by businesses sold by-owner.

Should sellers of small and midsize businesses sell by-owner . . . or list their business for sale with a business broker/intermediary? It depends. The book you are reading addresses this, and the implications for you.

You are up against two kinds of competitors.

You face two kinds of competitors, one more dangerous than the other.

- Individuals seeking business opportunities. There is a horde of unemployed or inexperienced buyers; they bid against each other to create a seller's market.

- Competitors of companies for sale. They want to "eat-to-beat" their competition. They realize that trying to grow their company by "fighting" their competition is the hard

way. Whenever they get a competitive advantage, their competitors copy them. When they "steal" their competitors'
customers or employees, competitors do the same to them.
When they launch a new marketing program, it takes time
and money before they know whether it succeeds or fails; acquiring or merging with a competitor adds marketing clout
and improves economies of scale. When done correctly, company growth by acquisition is faster, safer, cheaper and more
profitable than investing more time and money in marketing
to increase revenue.

Suspicious or contentious sellers.

What are business sellers are afraid of?

Sellers and their divestiture team, including business brokers,
rightfully are suspicious of "buyers." In their minds you are potentially dangerous until you prove yourself otherwise. Your acquisition
advisory team can help you establish your credibility.

Sellers of worthwhile companies are afraid that "buyers" are not
sufficiently prepared, motivated or qualified to buy. Sellers don't
want to waste time on so-called buyers who do not know how to
buy a business. Few sellers will tolerate buyers who want to hap-
hazardly evaluate the company for sale. All sellers want to know
whether or not the buyer is a wolf masquerading as a sheep, i.e. a
competitor or someone working for a competitor or another dangerous character. Sellers who will finance part of the purchase price
won't do so unless they believe the buyer can manage the company
at least as well as the exiting owner. When sellers say "show me your
money" wise buyers do so.

Kenneth H. Marks, founder and managing partner of High
Rock Partners, Inc., in "What issues are most contentious when selling a mid-market business?" published online by divestopedia.com
says: "The most contentious issue is the classic determining value
and agreement on the basis for the valuation of the business. The

other issue that goes right along with valuation is deferred or contingent consideration. In many cases, transactions will have some kind of consideration beyond the close, so an earnout, holdback or seller's note."

Why brokers and sellers don't follow up with buyers.

Too many buyers say: Why don't most brokers and sellers follow up with me? I have money and management experience!

Too many wannabe business buyers proceed half-cocked. Their amateur or disruptive approach to brokers and sellers repels opportunities. And then later, in some cases, when the new-and-improved buyer tries to reconnect to sellers and brokers, usually after getting around to assembling a worthwhile dealmaking advisory team, doors don't open. Buyers get one chance to make a favorable first impression.

Here's a fact of life: There are plenty of business buyers who know how to properly conduct themselves. That's why savvy brokers and sellers ignore the improperly prepared do-it-yourselfers or "buyers" who rely on the wrong kind of advisory team.

What sellers want to know—what they expect from you.

You may lose worthwhile opportunities if you fumble these inquiries from sellers.

- Your intent to buy *their* company.

- Your capacity to make a reasonable down payment and to guarantee installment payments on the balance of the purchase price that the seller, or another party, finances.

- Your promise to maintain the seller's and the business' confidentiality.

- Your experience managing a business (or supervising employees).

- Your ability to fit in with the company, its employees and its industry.

- Your history of successfully dealing with problems.

- Your integrity.

- Your leadership ability.

The unaware and the uninformed.

Sad but true: Too few businesses track and evaluate their performance and risk management metrics. And especially how their company's performance stacks up against competitors. Or alternative investments.

Pertaining to insurance coverage, financial results/trends, productivity, marketing, sales, employees, customers, vendors, product/service quality, competitors, reputation, online presence and business valuation.

You are going to have to look into those things. Do not overly rely on what the seller or the company tells you.

What lurks behind the Balance Sheet?

These things mean cash crunches. This can cause insolvency. This means bye-bye to your investment. So, What's lurking behind the Balance Sheet?

According to Investopedia.com, contingent liabilities need to pass two thresholds before they can be reported in the financial statements. It must be possible to estimate the value of the contingent liability and the liability must have a greater than 50% chance of being realized.

If the contingent loss has a less than 50% chance of occurring, the liability should not be reflected on the balance sheet but should be disclosed in the footnotes to the financial statements.

And that, folks, is what can bite buyers of companies. Who decides if the risk is likely or not, to what degree and at what cost?

Be sure you are aware of at least these four categories of liabilities and risk:

- Undisclosed

- Contingent

- Unfunded

- Potential

But the good news is . . . liabilities and risks are your opportunities for negotiation, thereby maximizing your safety and your return on investment.

The seller should provide various representations and warranties and then indemnify you for them, all of which is stipulated in your purchase contract.

Maybe the seller should pledge security to you if the unknown is too big. One technique is a reserve which the seller funds with enough cash or other assets for a specified time after closing against which you can draw to recoup excessive liabilities or accounts receivable bad debts.

What about a "right of offset" in your purchase contract? This can handle misunderstandings and undisclosed liabilities that become known to you after the business changes hands. The right of offset can be used to adjust the acquisition price and payments due (such as seller financing).

Don't overlook a holdback of funds provision. The buyer does not want the entire purchase price conveyed to the seller, especially some or all of the buyer's down payment; it is held in escrow pending transfer to the seller until certain events transpire, such as retention of key employees or customers.

So, what, specifically, lurks behind the Balance Sheet? Here are a few of 26 things buyers don't want to see in their rear-view mirror after their business merger or acquisition.

- Potential undisclosed pricing changes under current or renewing contracts

- Undisclosed recall or warranty claims

- Improper accruals

- Falsified documents to secure debt

- Financial statements have not been prepared consistently over the years, especially right now

And remember this: Too-few buyers put a reasonable price tag on these risks. For example: Accrued vacation and sick time for employees. What is the value of it? Must it be paid in cash to terminating employees? Who will do the work, at what additional cost, when employees consume their benefit?

How business sellers manipulate buyers.

Forewarned is forearmed. Manipulation can distort the receiving party's perception of reality.

When you understand what's going on in the minds of the people across from you at the dealmaking table you can better prepare and deploy your own counter measures.

Savvy sellers can manipulate buyers into buying the wrong company or acquiring the right company the wrong way. They can cause buyers to pay more than they should. They can cause naïve buyers to accept contractual provisions not in the buyer's self-interest.

- Do not misunderstand me. I am not referring to dishonest sellers. I'm referring to honest sellers that are better at negotiating than typical unknowing buyers.

An excerpt from Brad Tuttle's article in *Time Magazine*, "How You're Manipulated into Buying Stuff You Don't Want and Paying More Than You Should," states: "You'll buy when you think you're getting a deal, even when you're not. One of the oldest tricks in the book, according to a Pop Economics post at SmartSpending, is known as 'anchoring.' You're probably familiar with the idea, in which a high list price serves merely as a reference point so that the seller can grab the consumer's attention with something like '50% Discounts!' The truth is that the seller never really expects to sell the item at that artificial 'anchored' list price, and that it'd be happy to sell the item (at a decent profit) at the 'sale' price. The result is that many 'deals' are not good values."

And this, which can pertain to unemployed people wanting to buy a company, also from Brad Tuttle's article: "You're scared into buying via the 'fear tax.' As pointed out in a WiseBread post, we've all bought something basically because we were scared—of not looking good, of falling behind in our careers and technological savvy, of being looked down upon by neighbors and colleagues, of missing out on the latest amazing entertainment experience, of putting our families in harm's way, and so on. Marketers play up these fears, and society as a whole seems to willingly play along. But often, these fears are superficial and entirely unfounded."

Other tactics to manipulate buyers:

- the company just came on the market so act quickly before other buyers show up;

- there are not many companies like us or as good as us, and we're the only one for sale right now;

- hiding the company's history of previously being bought/ sold (such as to the present owner);

- rushing you through due diligence and dealmaking;

- ignoring deadlines;

- the price is going up soon because the seller is improving the company;

- other buyers are interested in the company for sale;

- identifying a common enemy and then "ally" with the buyer against it to get the buyer psyched up about buying the company instead of another company;

- you've revealed your hot buttons, which the seller is exploiting;

- good cop, bad cop where the seller is friendly, cooperative but seller representatives are not;

- limited authority, which occurs when the seller says "I wish I could but I cannot" without the approval of someone else;

- you must buy the company's real estate to buy the company;

- starting with unrealistic offers, which they easily give up to buyers who know how to obtain concessions, such as the asking price, terms of sale and anything else pertaining to the company or the potential buy/sell transaction;

- emotional influences designed to distract you from the facts, from reality;

- false flattery ("I can see that you have what it takes for success when you own my company.");

- pretending to be more like you than they really are ("I'm skeptical, too" and "I don't blame you for arguing");

- unreasonably minimizing your objections and concerns;

- unreasonable contract provisions;

- minimizing the value to you of the sellers' post-sale transitional assistance;

- withholding information and documents, which might be legal to do, which is why you need to know what you can reasonably request.

All these things might occur. But do not leap to the conclusion that someone is trying to fool you. Investigate. Collaborate. Negotiate. Pitch the advantages *you* bring to the dealmaking table and to the company.

When business seller financing is a sham.

Here's one of the things done by some sellers who believe their company is not worth buying.

It's not a good day for company owners to be told by business brokers and other kinds of professionals that their business is not marketable. Ethics-challenged owners try to dream up a convincing come-on. Something that unsuspecting buyers will fall for.

One juicy tactic has the owner touting "seller financing!" The seller will finance, say, 30% of the buyer's purchase price. The buyer borrows 50% of the purchase price from another source of financing. The buyer's down payment is only 20% of the price.

The seller, at closing, receives 70% of the sales price. (BTW, the price was probably higher than it would have been without seller financing.)

A few months later the buyer discovers the company is a horrible investment. The company may even be on its way to its demise.

The buyer ends up holding the bag, which among other things includes having to pay the business' debts (such as to other sources of financing that provided any of the acquisition or post-acquisition financing). Of course, the buyer threatens not to pay the seller the money due on the seller financing. The buyer might threaten to sue the former owner.

Now shift your gaze to the former owner. He did not care if he did not receive any payments from the buyer for the portion of the purchase the seller "financed." He sold an otherwise unsaleable company.

What about the buyer's threat of a lawsuit? The seller has the buyer's money (and the rest of the cash the seller received at closing plus the buyer's payments for the seller financing). These kinds of sellers defend themselves, if the buyer can find them, using the proceeds from their sale of the company.

Buyers in this predicament do not like the picture painted by litigators whom the buyer might hire to handle the lawsuit. The buyer, in reality, may not have enough money or courage to sue the former owner.

But what about buying a franchise?

According to an article published by Entrepreneur.com, *Where to Go When You Can't Find the Dough* (First hint: Start with your franchisor), "To keep their growth from stalling, many franchisors are offering unprecedented levels of franchisee assistance. Some are making loans themselves, while others are discounting franchise fees or letting new franchisees pay their fees over time. At the very least, your franchisor should help you beef up your loan paperwork. For instance, some franchisors are purchasing bank credit reports on their company from FRANdata, which explain franchisor financials and present the concept in a positive light."

These kinds of tactics can be worthwhile . . . if the franchise opportunity is worth buying.

DIY buyers are most susceptible to being taken. Savvy buyers employ a savvy acquisition team.

What about franchise resales?

Despite what some business buying advisors say, franchises should not be evaluated the same way as non-franchised (independent) companies. The franchisor provides and imposes opportunities and vulnerabilities on its franchisees. Online research will reveal to you the countless ways franchisors disappoint franchisees. That said, some franchises, properly acquired, can be a worthwhile investment, especially if the franchisor cannot impede their franchisees when the franchisees want to sell their franchise.

Any kind of company advertised for sale may not be a good deal for the buyer IF other buyers are also communicating with the seller.

Competition among buyers is good for sellers, not buyers. This is why we *Business Buyer Advocates* encourage buyers to search for businesses not for sale (but could be for sale if the right buyer inquires the right way). We also like businesses for sale by-owner; they rarely get the buyer-traffic that business brokers create for sellers.

We tell buyers to contact every broker in their locale, to see if the broker has a pocket listing (not advertised to the public) or maybe a new listing so our buyer can be the first to communicate with the seller.

Another good reason buyers should connect with brokers occurs when buyers have interest in a broker's listing that has been rejected by other buyers. Commonly, those sellers are dejected, and some of them are ready to do a deal. In these cases, the broker is almost on your team because the broker encourages the seller to seriously consider your offer. But, be careful: Brokers' primary loyalty is to their sellers.

Savvy buyers have their own advisory team; it does not include the seller's broker.

Things sellers do before you arrive on scene.

Sellers know it is easier to sell their company if it's a worthwhile investment.

Wise owners, before trying to sell their business, try to make it more attractive to buyers (and more profitable and enjoyable for themselves).

They want to increase the value of their company.

They realize almost nothing takes longer than trying to sell a business that is not ready for sale.

A few things owners do to increase the marketability and value of their company:

- They try to see their company as a buyer will view it. Focus is on the future. What will their business look like in a year?

- They improve their financial ratios to be in line with or better than the average of other businesses in their industry.

- They change their method of accounting to maximize the amount of profit the company reports.

- They make an effort to increase productivity (without adversely affecting employee morale).

- They review every expense; looking for ways to cut costs.

- They eliminate activities that have more downside risk than upside potential.

- They do not do anything that gives their business a short-term benefit at the expense of their business' future. (Buyers will detect short-term fixes that can impair the long-term, which means the company won't sell or it will sell for less than it would have if the owner was not so short-sighted.)

- They investigate opportunities to increase revenue and profit by adding products or another product line, or expanding geographically, or growing by acquiring another business, or diversifying their customer list and/or raising prices for the goods and services they sell.

Some companies deploy some of the 100+ business improvement projects, described in the "Internal Financing" section of my book: *How to Get ALL the Money You Want For Your Business Without Stealing It.* Most of these techniques are quick and easy to implement. Each one adds cash to the bottom line, which makes the company more marketable and valuable.

The playing field is tilted against buyers.

You cannot achieve the best deal possible if you play on an unlevel field.

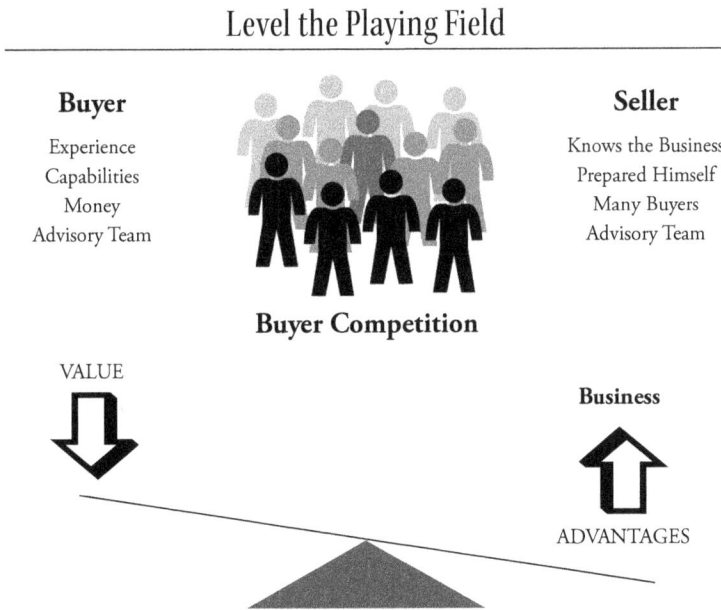

Level the Playing Field

Buyer

Experience
Capabilities
Money
Advisory Team

Seller

Knows the Business
Prepared Himself
Many Buyers
Advisory Team

Buyer Competition

VALUE

Business

ADVANTAGES

Not shown in the image above is the contribution business brokers add to the sellers' advantages. You will read about this throughout this book.

Do not misconstrue what you read in this book. It IS advisable for buyers, while searching for companies for sale, to stay in touch with brokers and other seller-intermediaries; doing so keeps buyers connected to sellers that might not appear while buyers are looking for businesses for sale by-owner on the hidden market.

Okay, so on with the story: You are a buyer. Out there are sellers. You want to buy a business. You have a problem. It's buyer competition.

Savvy buyers effectively access the hidden market because they want to avoid most, if not all, buyer competition. The hidden market is where to identify potential sellers, so the buyer can be first on scene. It is also where to find unadvertised businesses for sale by-owner. The hidden market can put you in touch with, depending upon the industry, up to 80% of the profitable companies that are sold (the keyword being "sold" versus for sale).

Start thinking in terms of US and THEM. Most observers say the playing field is tilted in the seller's favor. Buyers have an uphill climb.

Here's why sellers start with advantages:

1. They know more about their company and industry than you, and few will tell you everything;

2. They have prepared themselves and their company for sale;

3. They think there are a lot of buyers for it (which is often true);

4. They have an advisory team. And maybe a business broker represents them.

You have to know what you bring to the table, and effectively present it to sellers and their representatives:

1. Experience

2. Capabilities

3. Money

4. Acquisition advisory team.

This is your value. When the seller and the seller's team perceive your value as being worth the seller's business, a deal can take place and the business can change hands.

Phases and obstacles through which you must navigate.

The business broker's primary allegiance is to business sellers.

A Business Buyer Advocate levels the playing field for buyers using a proprietary Street-Smart 22-Step Acquisition Sequence ™.

A *Business Buyer Advocate* can help you navigate through:

1. Searching—so you meet more companies than you can find on your own.

2. Due diligence—evaluating the owner, the company and the transaction.

3. Financing—exploring creative financing & assessing sources of financing.

4. Pricing businesses for sale—pricing differs from valuation.

5. Dealmaking—doing what it takes to achieve a profitable done deal.

6. Post-acquisition due diligence and transition management.

No matter how experienced you are, these obstacles stand in the way of you buying a *worthwhile* business:

1. There is a horde of unemployed or inexperienced buyers; they bid against each other to create a *seller's* market.

2. Most businesses are not worth owning. Owners hope for a naive buyer.

3. Only 1 out of 5 of the <u>best</u> companies, which are sold, are advertised by sellers or offered through business brokers. (As you can imagine, statistics, like this one, vary depending upon the time, industry and the national and local economic conditions. You can easily Google the topic and find the array of data. When we counsel buyers, we tell them to take all stats with a large grain of salt,

which means what matters most is the degree to which worthwhile companies can be found to match a particular buyer's acquisition criteria. The figure we cite, here, has been most relevant to most of the buyers who hire us. Our buyers seek small and midsize companies for sale, not Main Street ventures or (usually) companies with annual revenue exceeding $10 million.)

4. Buyers who don't buy the right business the right way are disappointed in their purchase.

5. Being qualified to buy is not enough. You must know how to find winners and how to achieve a profitable done deal.

6. Depending upon the industry and type of buy/sell trans-action—where the seller and buyer reach agreement on everything else—up to 50% fail to close due to lack of acquisition financing, according to a national survey.

How business buyers are blindsided by the seller's employees.

Savvy business buyers detect insights from the employees of companies for sale—before they purchase the business.

Buyer interactions with employees are crucial, especially during due diligence. But too many buyers cause too much trouble. And too many people on the dealmaking playing field do not know how to adequately handle such interactions.

One of the most popular TeleSeminars I've presented reveals how business buyers are blindsided by the seller's employees, and how to avoid it.

I'm calling your attention to the interactions between business buyers and the employees of companies for sale because buyers cannot see the company as it really is by only talking to owners and managers. They simply don't see it as it is. They're busy handling day-to-day activity and putting out fires. They don't have time to step back and see their business for what it really is—every strength that gives it a competitive advantage, and the actual or pending vulnerabilities that threaten its future.

Those of you who've been on the dealmaking playing field for a while know the risks that may arise. And you also know . . . whether or not you like it . . . that some business buyers will communicate with employees, and sometimes they'll do it without the seller's permission.

Worse, too many buyers don't know when and how to communicate with the seller's employees, even when they get the seller's permission.

I don't know any professional advisors that tell buyers: You can't and shouldn't, before buying a business, interview any of the seller's employees.

In fact, professional advisors tell buyers that due diligence includes learning about the attitudes, opinions and intentions of the employees, from the employees themselves, especially the key employees.

Buyers, sellers and their representatives, rightfully, fear interaction between buyers and the seller's employees; it is fraught with legal and business risk. The good news is that win-win deals can occur when people correctly handle this touchy topic.

The sad truth is quite a few sellers don't have a clue about what it takes to close win-win transactions.

Buyers and sellers need to know how to safely handle permissible interactions between buyers and employees.

If buyers don't interact with the seller's employees, good luck!

Interviewing the seller's employees.

One of the major reasons why so many buyers suffer bad deals is their failure to adequately investigate small and midsize companies for sale . . . from the perspective of a company insider.

The employees of companies for sale can be the buyer's best reality check.

You can discover the real reason for sale. You can materially improve negotiations.

Some owners decide to sell their company upon learning that a key employee may quit and then compete with the company. Some (but not all) sellers disclose this possibility to prospective business buyers.

A while back, a client met the owner of a business doing $3,500,000 a year in sales. The company was started in 1910. It was being run by the grandson of the deceased founder. The grandson started putting lots of the business' profits up his nose. The business could afford his drug habit, but it could not afford his lack of attention to business while he was high. Profits were declining. Employees were jumping ship because they saw their future was at risk. My client saved the day.

He had two things the owner desperately needed: (1) He wasn't a drug addict, and (2) He knew how to manage and grow a business.

My client got 51% control of this business without purchasing even 1% of the stock. He owned 51% of the stock if he stopped the company from losing ground. Not grow, but simply stop the slide. Why would the seller agree to this? Because he was faced with losing it all.

Why could my client get this opportunity? Because he knew how.

It is not easy to find one of these deals. In fact, without a very specific search system it's nearly impossible to find one. And when you find one, you must know exactly what to do, in the correct sequence. You must act very quickly, or somebody else gets the deal.

The personnel of a business can be its most significant asset. There may be actual or latent problems that can undermine the company.

Involve a labor attorney if you suspect red flags, such as the company's failure to fund or comply with pension and profit sharing plans, grant employee changes in compensation and perks according to what has been promised, compliance with union agreements and governmental rules and regulations, the company's failure to remit payroll taxes to taxing jurisdictions, present and former employees' compliance with nondisclosure agreements and covenants not to compete, and whether or not there have been or probably will be employees who claim the company mistreated them.

Buyers start in second gear when they take over a company with disgruntled employees.

The worst case we've seen happened to the buyer of a print shop. Within one month of the buyer taking over, the salesman, production manager and office manager quit. The new owner, who was a former corporate autocrat, had berated these employees, saying they were like sheep that needed his direction to accomplish anything. For payback with style, these people walked out the door for the last time wearing plastic sheep masks. They leased space across the street, so it was easy for customers to see the new competition. It took the buyer about one year to go out of business and then another year to wrap up his divorce.

Probe key employees for business and industry intelligence that you can use to manage the business or a similar company you buy. And then, after you buy a business, you can go back to employees working for the company you did not buy if you want them to work for you, especially if their capability is better than what is available in the business you bought.

Asking naive questions invites misdirection.

When you interview the key employees, with the seller's advance written permission, don't merely ask if they are happy with their relationship with the seller's company. Ask whether they intend to retain their relationship on the present terms. And if not, why not? Maybe ask: Why do you choose to work for this company?

Don't ignore the reputations of key stakeholders. Ask the employees about the reputation and reliability of the company's key customers, employees, landlord, sources of financing and suppliers.

Don't forget to search online for info about the seller, the company and its key employees, customers, suppliers, etcetera.

Discover the seller's promises to employees. Is there an agreement between the owner and any employee that provides a benefit to the employee upon the sale of the business?

Consider these questions:

1. How important is it to interview the seller's employees?

2. What are the most important questions to ask employees?

3. What typical ways are new owners blindsided by employees?

4. What about conflicts or integration of my business capabilities with the company's employees?

5. Can I rely upon what employees tell me about the company?

6. What HR matters should my attorney review?

7. Should I be worried about differing perspectives of employees I interview (i.e., cheerful or unhappy, optimistic or pessimistic)?

8. What red flags should I avoid?

9. What about contacting former employees?

10. What can buyers gain or lose when talking to company employees without the seller's permission?

11. What's the best way to convince sellers to let me interview employees?

12. What kinds of employees are the best to interview?

13. How can I discover if there are people working for the company but not being paid or not being paid by the seller's company?

14. How can I learn about the company's history with theft or embezzlement?

15. Are there actual or latent costs relating to employees that may not show up on the business' books?

16. What about applicable governmental licenses, training or education requirements?

17. How can I evaluate the capability and integrity of key employees?

18. How can I zero in on the company's organizational and cultural attributes?

19. How can I compare my managerial style to how the company has been managed?

20. What about post-sale retention of employees?

You can read the detailed explanations and recommendations for those questions in my book: *How to Buy the Right Business the Right Way—Dos, Don'ts & Profit Strategies*. It's available from my website.

This information can educate people who want to achieve a done deal; it can also help their advisors.

Think about the perspective of sellers.

It is not easy for sellers to identify the best time to sell their company. Why risk money, and the blood, sweat and tears sellers have invested in their business? When it's time to cash out, they must know how to get out—quickly—without leaving money on the table. It takes preparation and timing. Business transfer intermediaries and other professional advisors can show them how to do both, so sellers get the best deal.

There is a "best" buyer, but most sellers are not good enough at articulating this, so they waste time and money. They risk their company's confidentiality communicating with the wrong kinds of "buyers."

Companies sell more quickly and on better terms if sellers communicate with buyers who do not pose a competitive threat. (On the other hand, properly handled, competitors can be a ready, able and willing potential buyer.)

Savvy sellers want to attract buyers who are actively searching for a business like theirs. Street-smart sellers find out early in their communications whether buyers have sufficient financial and managerial capability to buy and then run their business—right now.

Business transfer intermediaries and other professional advisors show sellers how to excite buyers about their company (without identifying it too soon) and how to screen buyers before sellers reveal trade secrets.

Few company owners know enough about the process to sell a business.

Apocalypse Underway for Retail Businesses

Listen up! Business buyers, sellers, business brokers, insurance agents, landlords, suppliers, customers, employees, investors, sources of financing.

Retailers. You're at risk if you own one. You're at risk if you're the last owner holding the bag when your business goes kaput. You're at risk if your income depends upon retailers.

Mounting losses and closures are adversely affecting segments of the retail industry, some more than others. And it will get worse. Tangible product purveyors are more at risk than service providers (until we can get a massage or haircut on Amazon).

Retailers represent the largest, by far, sector of the various kinds of U.S. establishments. About 10% of the total in 2017, down every year for quite a few years. Nearly 99% of retail businesses employ fewer than 50 people.

Looking at some of the businesses-for-sale websites it seems that of the kinds of businesses for sale retailers make up about 13% of the total. The point, here, is that on a proportional basis, there are 30% more businesses for sale among retailers, themselves, compared to retailers accounting for 10% of the total kinds of businesses.

Does this suggest that retail shop owners are selling to greater fools to avoid upcoming losses? (Okay, for you stat hounds, it's not the percentages to focus on here; it's what is happening and going to happen to retailers.)

I'm not going to tell you the "whys" for it. Google the topic. I'm simply warning you to beware and be aware before you venture into certain parts of the retail segment.

Remember mom-and-pop VHS and then DVD rental shops? What about music stores, photo shops, florists, computer stores, book stores, gift/novelty shops, shoe shops, clothing stores?

What about these chains?

A&P, Abercrombie & Fitch, Al's Auto Supply, American Apparel, B. Dalton, Blockbuster, Bombay, Borders Books, Circuit City, Coldwater Creek, Cole Haan, CompUSA, Contractor Supply, Daffy's, Deb, Delia's, F.A.O. Schwarz, Filene's Basement, Florsheim Shoes, GameStop, Gander Mountain, Golfsmith, Gymboree, hhgregg, J.C. Penney, KB Toys, Kmart, Levitz Furniture, Linens-n-Things, Loehmann's, Lumberjack Building Materials, Macy's, Mervyn's, OfficeMax, PacSun, Pay 'N Pak, Quiksilver, RadioShack, Rexall, Sears, Sound Advice, Sports Authority, Staples, The Limited, Tower Records, Toys"R"Us, True Religion, Urban Outfitters, Wet Seal, Woolworth.

It's not a pretty picture for many sellers.

The buy/sell experience is not a pretty picture for sellers that take the typical course. It partially explains the cynical attitude of some sellers.

Industry experts know these things, some of which is known by sellers:

- Dozens of buyers, on average, contact each seller of a profitable business.

- Some "buyers" string along unsuspecting sellers—to practice their buying technique—knowing they will not buy from the seller with whom they are rehearsing and from which they are gathering industry intelligence.

- 95% of "buyers" never buy.

- Many deals fall apart in escrow because of unrealistic sellers and buyers.

- Only 20% of businesses for sale ever sell (depending on size and industry).

- Many sellers think they settled for too big a discount of their asking price.

As if this is not discouraging enough for the uninformed business seller, we have observed that 50% of buyers back out of deals because they are not confident the seller knows enough about how to sell a business, or because the buyer is not sure the seller is fully and honestly disclosing information.

Who is selling whom?

Most people are nervous about business buying and the negotiating that occurs on the way to a done deal. But what most buyers don't know is this: It is much more difficult for the seller to convince you to make an offer and then buy the company than it is for you to put to your advantage what you learn about the seller and the company. You are playing offence; they are defending. And it would be that way except for this: The best brokers are master salespeople. And so are many sellers. They can turn the table on you, flustering you so you don't consistently play to your advantage.

Now is a good time to remind yourself about the Golden Rule. Not this one . . . "do unto others what you would like to be done to you." That is a good rule. Playing fairly is a good way to build trust along the pathway to a win-win done deal.

But right now, think about this: Whoever has the gold makes the rules! Without the money you bring to the dealmaking table there would be no deal. Don't forget it. And don't let sellers and brokers forget it. Be nice about it but the other side should realize that unless they behave in ways that satisfy you, you will take your money to another table. Be reasonable but don't let them cause you to think you need their company more than they want your money.

Buyer competition is key—for sellers.

Buyer competition creates a seller's market, which maximizes price, quickens the sale and lessens haggling.

Mike Handelsman, general manager, BizBuySell.com, writes, "Create a bidding war. Almost everyone knows someone who sold a house above the asking price because more than one buyer expressed interest at the same time. It's possible to create a similar scenario in the sale of a business, but to do it the seller needs to maximize the attention the business receives in the marketplace. One of the best ways to maximize exposure is to list the sale online. The majority of small business buyers conduct their search themselves, and increasingly, the place they do so is on the internet. By listing online, sellers have the ability to customize their listing in ways that can make it truly attractive and boost visibility to stir up competitive interest among buyers, all of which can give the seller the ultimate upperhand in negotiations."

When competition is good . . . and not good . . . for you.

Let's focus on the buying and selling of small and midsize businesses.

Savvy company owners and their brokers create a seller's market by attracting multiple buyers who must compete with one another.

Sometimes the dumbest buyer wins the bidding war. (Of course, this is wonderful if you're a seller.)

So, what's a buyer to do? Look for competition posed by sellers of other companies. It doesn't have to be the same kind of company with which you are negotiating. When the time is right, discreetly and tactfully let the other side of your dealmaking table know they aren't the only game in town.

Another way to beat buyer competition is to be the seller's first choice among the field of buyers. You do that by properly handling yourself with the seller and the seller's representatives. Don't be obnoxious. Collaboration is better than head-butting.

Say to the seller: What if I do such-and-such? How can you reciprocate? Or this: What can we do to make a win-win deal?

We *Business Buyer Advocates* have dozens of techniques to disarm or create competition so our clients can achieve worthwhile done deals.

Inside the buyers' minds.

Savvy sellers discover a few things about buyers, which sellers exploit to their advantage. They focus on the buyer's psyche while the buyer focuses on the seller's company.

According to a survey conducted by Opinion Research Inc., the desire to get rich was cited by only 9% of people who want to become a business owner.

The strongest reasons for wanting to own a business: "doing something I love" and "security."

So adept sellers and brokers showcase the *enjoyment* the company offers. They appeal to the buyer's desire to "do something I love."

Sellers and brokers stimulate the buyer's need for *security*, showing how the company can provide permanence of employment and financial security.

Safety is more important to most buyers than profit—no matter what buyers say.

Most buyers won't buy an unprofitable business, but many buyers will purchase a business whose profit has been less than the buyer initially wants if the buyer believes the business is not about to suffer a downturn.

Studies say security is the fundamental, universal reason why people want to own a business.

A "buyer" who is willing to take the risk of buying a business does so because of his/her belief that the only real security from a job is the job that he/she creates in the company he/she owns. A wise business seller subtly encourages buyers to fully understand this. Buyers who have lost or hate their job see the truth in this.

Companies that have been sold knew how to position their business for sale, showcasing its benefits, opportunity and stability.

Good deal or a dumb deal?

Below are some of the topics that determine the degree to which you are going to make a good deal or a dumb deal.

This book and your advisory team can show you what's important and how to dig deeper.

Historical Pretax Net Profit

Prior earnings usually are the most reliable guide as to the future expectancy. (IRS Revenue Ruling 59-60)

Historical performance is important, but not as important as where the business is going and how much profit it will earn.

Terms of Sale

The provisions of the buy/sell contract: defining characteristics, elements and structure of the transaction.

Continuity of Profit

Likelihood that the company will maintain its historical profit level without interruption into the foreseeable future, taking into account change of ownership, industry trends, etc.

Competition

"Two guys are walking through the jungle when a lion appears on the path ahead of them. One of the two starts putting on a pair of running shoes. 'Why bother with running shoes?' says the first guy. 'There's no way you can outrun a lion.' 'Who said anything about outrunning a lion? says the second. 'I just want to outrun you.'" Ichak Adizes

Company Competitive Advantage

Warren Buffett says the most important thing he looks for when evaluating a company is its "sustainable competitive advantage."

Industry

There are no worst types of business—but a particular business may not be worth buying. You can make a street-smart investment by acquiring a strong company in a temporarily troubled or declining industry.

Company Growth—Actual & Potential

Some businesses are for sale because the owner does not want to make an additional investment for more production capacity. Business buyers frequently overestimate the production capacity, only to discover after buying the business that it is under a low ceiling for growth.

Marketability

Don't confuse marketability with value. What if too-few buyers want to purchase the *type* of business you want to buy? You could pay a "fair" price only to discover that you can't sell your business when you need to sell it.

Type of Company

Be open-minded. Just because a particular type of business appeals to you does not mean you should forego looking at others.

Location

Location! Location! Location!

Premises and other Tangible Assets

How much will they contribute to or detract from the success of the company?

Type of Management the Company Requires from its Owner

Don't underestimate the amount of oversight that it takes to manage a company. Owners of small businesses (except the one you want to buy) will tell you that "passive management" is an oxymoron.

Intangible Enhancer to or Detractor from Value

Goodwill, ill-will and intellectual property are intangible. Don't assume the business has goodwill. If a seller cannot present a buyer with a credible rationale for the value of the business' goodwill, the buyer calls it blue sky. Then the argument begins. Don't let goodwill mask ill-will.

Economic Outlook

Local and national economy as it pertains to the company *and* its customers *and* its suppliers.

Restrictive Agreements

Watch out for restrictive agreements, especially poorly conceived ones that invite unintended legal and tax consequences. The more severe the restrictions, the higher the (downward) adjustment to value.

Don't conflate goodwill with good luck.

What should you know about valuing goodwill?
Don't conflate goodwill with good luck.

The IRS defines goodwill as the difference between the selling price of a business and the value of the tangible assets that buyers purchase.

Beware of goodwill, especially if its basis is the owner's business relationships with the company's customers, employees, landlord, bank and suppliers. To what degree can you reasonably expect to match or surpass the quality of the seller's?

Don't buy unverifiable "potential."

Just because a business has been profitable is not enough reason to buy it. Relying too much on historical performance is like looking into a rearview mirror to see what is ahead.

Buy an independent, mature, profitable business with a good future if you want to win bigger. You'll make money from DAY ONE.

My book, *How to Buy the Right Business the Right Way*, delves deeply into this topic because too many business buyers run out of luck thanks to the nonsense they believed about the company before acquiring or merging with it.

Valuation nonsense from brokers and sellers.

You can cut through the "valuation" nonsense from brokers and sellers.

Access *reliable* statistics about the asking prices, sales prices and terms of sale for the kinds, sizes and locations of "comparable" businesses. Numerous third-party (i.e., independent) databases report this kind of data.

Don't rely on the opinion of any single source of "valuation."

The easiest way for brokers and sellers to "get real" about valuation is to show facts to them. Of course, some people don't want to be confused by the facts. In which case you can move on to another potential deal.

Business brokers, other business transfer intermediaries.

There are several kinds of business transfer intermediaries, but let's for our convenience lump them into a job title everyone recognizes: "Business Broker."

"Business Broker" is defined by investopedia.com as a professional who specializes in the purchase and sale of companies. Transferring ownership of a business is a complex process involving determining a fair price for the company, making sure the business's finances and financial records are in order, negotiating a price, going through escrow and closing the sale. Business brokers not only manage these steps, but also ensure confidentiality by requiring interested buyers to agree not to disclose the details of the potential business sale. Business brokers can also help with licensing and permitting requirements and can weed out unqualified buyers.

Business brokers are salespeople. Their job is to sell businesses. They sell you on the features and benefits of the companies they represent. Sellers pay brokers a sales commission, which is due and payable upon closing of the buy/sell transaction. Other ways some brokers are compensated by sellers include fees for helping the owner prepare the company for sale or performing an appraisal of value.

Business brokers make possible the exchange of small and midsize companies that might not otherwise occur. Few owners of wonderful companies know how or have the time to market their business for sale; few know how to handle the complexities of deal-making. One of the best decisions company owners make is deciding to list their business for sale with a business broker.

The Great Recession wreaked havoc among business brokers, as it did to the entire business community. Fewer owners were willing to sell their company in a market characterized by declining revenue and profit, worried buyers, lack of institutional financing and an uncertain economic future.

The brokers surviving the Great Recession generally are good salespeople; they had to be to make money during the downturn.

Some of them did what other people in business do when profit is threatened: They diversified into other professional services.

"Why do sellers hire business brokers instead of trying to sell by-owner? That was the title of a poll taken a few years ago. Respondents included company owners and professional advisors to small and midsize businesses. Results of the poll appear in my report, "62 Reasons for Sellers Hiring Brokers." The report itemizes the contributions business brokers add to the sellers' advantages. You can see the report by searching online for it; numerous brokerage firms, for example, post it on their websites.

The main reasons why sellers hire business transfer intermediaries:

1. Intermediaries understand and can depersonalize negotiations.

2. Intermediaries know how to sell businesses; most sellers don't.

3. Intermediary compensation is usually or mostly contingent upon the sale.

4. Most buyers start with business brokers and Internet searches.

5. Intermediaries understand local marketplaces of businesses for sale.

6. Intermediaries understand and can explain to buyers the seller's industry.

Business transfer intermediaries of all types function as go-betweens; they can filter communications so all parties to the pending transaction can focus on the most salient points and realistically negotiate differences of opinion. It is normal for conflicts to arise between sellers and buyers (and their advisors). Sometimes it pertains to personalities; and maybe differing goals or misunderstandings about facts. The best business transfer intermediaries can help people understand the facts and find win-win compromises instead of becoming unnecessarily defensive.

Search on my website, PartnerOnCall.com, to see the full report: *62 Reasons for Sellers Hiring Brokers*.

And then think about the kind of advisory team that can help you cope with the advantages that brokers and other kinds intermediaries convey to sellers.

My view of business brokers.

If you have been looking for a business to buy you may have strong opinions about business brokers. You may have interacted with a few brokers, maybe a dozen of them. Perhaps what you have experienced is not indicative of the brokerage profession if you have not been satisfied with your encounters with brokers. What I've seen may challenge your perception of brokers, especially if you have not worked with any of the best brokers.

I've interacted with more than two thousand brokers during my four decades of dealmaking. I've attended their seminars and conventions. I've presented workshops and speeches to groups of brokers. I've collaborated with more than two hundred of them on behalf of business buyers who hired me. 1,500 brokers receive my e-newsletters. Numerous brokers regularly exchange ideas with me.

Working the other side of the dealmaking table on behalf of buyers gives me an inside view into business brokerage. Most of them have done a superb job serving their seller clients. Most of them collaborate well, on behalf of sellers, when they interact with buyers as long as the buyers come properly prepared to buy a business, which includes being reasonable during due diligence, valuation and dealmaking.

Business Buyer Advocates benefit business brokers.

The goal of a *Business Buyer Advocate* is to facilitate the safe and profitable transfer of businesses, as quickly as possible—so every party to the transaction gets a win-win deal.

Problems brokers face.

Here are a few of the long-lasting problems with which business brokers cope. These challenges will probably forever be present. That's why we show you how we help brokers (and other M&A intermediaries) convert challenges into opportunities, which result in more win-win-win done deals. The parties to the buy/sell transaction win and so do the business brokers and the *Business Buyer Advocate*.

Not enough good sellers:

Actually, there are plenty of mature, profitable and fairly priced businesses for sale. Many of these businesses are for sale by-owner. Few of these owners advertise the business for sale. They don't have to. Some of these sellers contact "Partner" On-Call Network. If one of our *Business Buyer Advocates* represents a buyer whose acquisition criterion matches the seller's company, we introduce our buyer to the seller.

If our buyer does not purchase the company, we determine whether the owner is more likely to sell the company with the help of a business broker instead of continuing to try to sell by-owner. If so, we refer the seller to business brokers with whom we have a reciprocal referral relationship. Were it not for our strong recommendation that the owner employ a business broker, it is unlikely the owner would list the business for sale with any broker.

Difficulty finding financing:

Business brokers in the USA, Canada, the U.K, and elsewhere use my creative financing book to close deals: *How to Get ALL the Money You Want For Your Business Without Stealing It.*

Deal Killers: Attorneys & CPAs?

The best attorneys and accountants kill dumb deals. And they should.

What irritates brokers, buyers and sellers are the few attorneys and accountants that kill deals because these advisors don't know enough about dealmaking to protect their client AND facilitate a done deal.

The few professional advisors who venture into dealmaking, which is not their forte, do so because their client does not know advisors who can facilitate a done deal. Business buyers and sellers are wise to access advisors who have all the insight the buyer/seller needs to make an informed decision. Business brokers, who don't want deal killers to obstruct what could be a good done deal, sometimes refer their business buyer to a *Business Buyer Advocate*. We provide business guidance that supplements the specialty involvement by attorneys, accountants, business appraisers and sources of financing.

Because we network with specialty advisors whose reputation is getting the deal done, we can refer the buyer to these specialists.

Corporate people have no idea how to buy or run a small business:

It's true. Most former corporate executives have difficulty "pulling the trigger" when they find a business good enough to buy. And some of these managers find it difficult to transfer their big company experience into a small or midsize business.

Post-Acquisition Planning & Management is how we help buyers transition into a good company so the new owner does not inadvertently undermine the success of the business.

Price contention:

It's normal for buyers and sellers to be suspicious of each other's opinion about the value of a business for sale. No matter how honest and competent the business broker, a prudent buyer will listen to the broker's pitch with a large grain of salt.

Business Buyer Advocates have for decades observed good and bad deals. We've participated in countless done deals where the seller of a mature, profitable company transferred it to a buyer who was delighted with the purchase terms and then successfully managed the company.

Business brokers refer buyers AND sellers to us because of our street-smart experience and our access to buy/sell stats that we get from numerous databases that collect information about done deals.

As necessary, we connect the buyer or seller to an independent third-party pricing specialist who can provide a credible price fairness opinion or a business valuation.

Our involvement can avert or eliminate the inevitable argument between a genuine seller and buyer. Our involvement can also support the buyer's application for financing (which today is more important than ever).

Unprepared sellers:

Too many brokers waste too much time and money trying to sell companies that are not adequately prepared for sale.

According to article in *The Wall Street Journal*. "Want to Sell a Business? You May Not Be Ready," seven of ten midsize businesses will transfer ownership during the next decade, and at least 90% are now ill-prepared. For their part, buyers are getting more demanding than ever. "What Wall Street has been used to is now coming to Main Street, in that the same type of care is taken with these transactions."

"Partner" On-Call Network works with business brokers to prepare companies for sale. This makes the business easier to sell, so the broker makes more profit and has a happier client.

Brokers competing with brokers:

Brokers don't like having business buyers, whom the broker can't serve, go to competing brokers. Instead of brokers benefiting their competition, which occurs when a buyer the broker can't serve goes to another broker, some of the best brokers refer these buyers (which they are going to lose anyway) to a *Business Buyer Advocate* trained by "Partner" On-Call Network.

We conduct a custom search for buyers, introducing them to the best businesses for sale by-owner, ones buyers cannot find on their own.

While we're working the businesses for sale by-owner marketplace, these brokers keep trying to list a business that meets the buyer's acquisition criteria. The client returns to the broker to evaluate the company, using our proprietary system: *The Street-Smart Way to Buy a Business* ®. This enables all parties to expedite the process of dealmaking.

Wasting time on buyers:

According to the newsletter, *The Business Broker*, August 2007, "nine out of ten [buyers] are time-wasters." (Not much has changed since 2007!) The newsletter explains numerous ways business brokers can screen and serve buyers without creating a conflict of interest. Business brokers that refer buyers to a *Business Buyer Advocate* for buyer training will know the buyer is serious. After training, the broker works with a motivated buyer who has reasonable expectations and less fear of failure.

Conflict of interest:

The primary objective of most business brokers, especially the most astute brokers, is to list good businesses for sale and then create buyer competition so the companies the brokers represent sell on terms that favor their client, which is the seller. However, a few business brokers and other types of M&A intermediaries additionally offer consulting service to business buyers. This activity raises the concern of conflict of interest in the mind of some buyers and professional advisors within the buy/sell industry.

There are other reasons why business brokers refer some of their most serious buyers to *"Partner" On-Call Network*. We can provide the third-party verification the buyer needs to know a deal is worth doing—and then we can stay on the buyer's team after the deal closes.

Who is trying to sell to you?

Think about the process most people use to buy a car. Besides deciding what kind of car and its features (i.e., acquisition criteria), we research the marketplace. We want to know the best places to find the best deal; we want to know the tricks salespeople will try to pull on us; we want to know the dealers' costs and profit margins; we want to know how they will bait us into their offering and then romance us to our purchase. Try to transfer that example into the realm of business buying.

Pricing businesses for sale.

Sellers of small and midsize businesses may not *need* to hire an independent appraiser to value the business enterprise or its assets. But sellers might *want* to do so. Professional guidance can be the irrefutable remedy when a seller, broker, buyer or source of financing disagrees on the selling price for the business.

Appraisers are not the only source of credible information, which sellers can use to price businesses for sale. Some business transfer intermediaries and other professional advisors access national databases containing business sale statistics. This enables sellers to price their business from many points of view. This technique gives sellers more flexibility when they decide on their asking price and the terms of sale. Actual sales price information from credible third parties is a powerful persuader when a buyer asks sellers to justify the sellers' price.

Preparing the seller and the company for sale.

One of the most difficult tasks that sellers face, besides discovering how a buyer will perceive the seller's business, is to know which weak parts of the business to correct. Some improvements are more important. Prioritizing change is critical because each improvement can impact the business in many ways. Business transfer intermediaries and other professional advisors can help sellers identify the business' weak links. And then recommend only the essential changes in a sequence that has maximum impact—so sellers get the biggest bang for their buck.

Sellers hire business transfer intermediaries and/or other professional advisors for guidance that helps sellers achieve goals:

- Coach sellers to answer buyers' questions and concerns.

- Compile necessary information about the company.

- Refer sellers to accountants, appraisers, brokers and lawyers.

- Determine best time to offer the company for sale.

- Develop the marketing strategy and plan its implementation.

- Maximize the price buyers will pay for the business.

- Minimize interference with seller's management of company.

- Negotiating strategy.

- Prepare two versions of the business profile (teaser and full).

- Prepare the owner to sell and prepare company for sale.

- Reconcile differences between tax returns and financial statements.

- Get a higher price than the seller going it alone could get.

Merchandising businesses for sale.

Failure to properly package or merchandise the business for sale causes it to take longer to sell (if it sells), and it will sell for less money on less desirable terms. Most business owners are good at managing their company, but it is the rare owner who is expert at managing the sale of a business. When sellers attempt to deal directly with a buyer, the buyer discounts virtually everything the seller asserts, unless an independent third party has participated in the gathering and analysis of information about the seller's business.

Business transfer intermediaries and other professional advisors can establish a strategy to market the seller's business. They can help prepare written sales materials, such as an offering prospectus; they can estimate the most probable price range within which the business will sell. Business transfer intermediaries and other professional advisors can teach sellers how to answer questions the buyer will pose, and advise what questions sellers should ask buyers. If sellers want to hire a broker, professional advisors can show sellers how to select the right one for the seller's type of company.

Analysis of purchase offers.

Business transfer intermediaries and other professional advisors can critique purchase offers. They can identify areas where sellers should pay particular attention in structuring a counteroffer or preparing the contract of sale. They can also prepare, for the company and the seller, an estimate of net proceeds of sale and a post-sale cash flow analysis.

Dealmaking.

Tasks performed by business transfer intermediaries and/or other professional advisors include:

- Assistance during escrow closing.

- Background check on potential buyers run by broker or advisor.

- Broker or advisor can confer with seller, legal and tax counsel about terms of sale.

- Continual followup with buyers for decisions.

- Control buyers: Brokers and some advisors know what is appropriate and inappropriate.

- Deals almost die numerous times; Brokers and some advisors know how to revive them.

- Explain and handhold seller throughout selling process.

- Help buyer obtain financing.

- Mediate and negotiate with buyers.

- Receive, present and help evaluate purchase offers.

- Unsolicited offers from buyers require expert help.

You must pleasantly upset sellers.

It's not easy to find the best opportunities. Especially if you don't include searching on the hidden market of companies not yet for sale and for sale by-owner. Finding several of the best kinds of businesses for you is easier than achieving a done deal.

Sellers and their advisors are set in their ways, long before they encounter you. Their preparation and pitch to sell their company fuels their perspectives, behaviors and objectives when you come along.

That's why savvy buyers (and savvy advisors) from the get-go try to widen the perspectives of sellers and their representatives.

Most sellers have not adequately looked into their company and their offering the ways buyers do. You can delicately, for sellers, hold up a mirror that reflects how outsiders (buyers, investors and sources of financing) see their company.

Here are a few things you can do to enable sellers to see it as it is:

- If you are already financially and managerially capable of buying and successfully managing the company, present your credentials upfront. (Most people are not adequately prepared nor capable of buying and managing a company; sellers are sick and tired of these poseurs.)

- Softly upset sellers and their representatives. But first let them speak their piece on every topic. Gently tell it like it is and diplomatically ask questions and request documents, interviews, whatever.

- Consider handing the seller a letter, which reads like a personal (not business) communication. Express things from a human view; this can sand off what otherwise can be rough edges that may offend sellers.

- Propose supportable offers. Don't lowball. Explain your rationale; be reasonable; show evidence that sellers can verify. This will go a long way toward receiving better counter offers.

- Focus on and let the seller know you are focusing on the opportunities the business can convey to you. Don't infer to sellers that their baby is ugly. Warren Buffett says, "Price is what you pay; value is what you get."

- Sometimes walking away from the deal is the best way to make the deal. If you try this, the seller is more likely to welcome you back if you share your disappointment as you walk away. "I really wish we could agree."

Before you blame advisors, read this chapter so you see how easy it is for buyers and sellers, themselves, to kill their pending transactions.

This chapter is for professional advisors and people who want to know what professionals know.

Please read this chapter before hiring your advisory team. And, perhaps, share it with them, too.

As to selecting your advisory team: Hire people with a proven history of working for buyers and sellers of the *kind and size* of deal you intend. Ask how they have *facilitated* deals that *should* and *did* occur.

Hire dealmakers, deal closers.

In this chapter I'm going to reveal things that can destroy *worthwhile* transactions, but first, again, let's focus on selecting your advisory team:

- Hire people with a proven history of working for *buyers and sellers* of the kind and size of deal you intend.

- Ask how they have *facilitated* deals that *should* and *did* occur.

- Hire dealmakers, deal closers.

Avoid the *wrong* kind of deal killer. There are two kinds of deal killers:

- There are advisors who don't know enough about dealmaking for small and midsize companies. Not wanting to make mistakes these poseurs are more likely to poo-poo deals or, worse, bless them.

- The other kind of deal killer is adequately experienced, which means when they try to kill the deal, do it.

Planning for the best. Coping with the worst.

There is a big difference between attorneys who advise on transactions instead of litigation. While someday you might become embroiled in disputes and litigation, if right now you want to sell, acquire or merge a company, a "transactional attorney" may be more likely to see and facilitate the upside of your business potential and protect your downside on the basis of having helped clients achieve win-win done deals.

Similarly, you can get a better result if all the members of your advisory have a future-focus; if they can help you discover and exploit opportunities instead of turning every potential risk into a life-threatening situation. Sure, it's important to detect vulnerabilities. And the best advisors can show you how to fix or live with them within an already-profitable company.

Sandbagging during dealmaking and post-closing.

I'm sharing this topic with you because few dealmakers and advisors are adequately informed about sandbagging. I think buyers, sellers and their representatives need to see this information. Please don't blame the messenger (me) for this reality check. I do not advocate for sandbagging, but it happens more than we like. Your attorney can tell you horror stories.

Sandbagging is a coercive tactic during a pending buy/sell transaction. It can also be used post-closing to hurt the seller or buyer.

What does sandbagging mean? Why do people do it?

Sandbagging delays negotiations and/or a business deal. It can include misdirection, withholding and bluffing. It can unfairly disadvantage the other side of the dealmaking table.

Sandbagging is a behavior that can give the *buyer* the right to make an indemnity claim after closing for an inaccurate fact that a buyer *knew* was false when signing the document, despite *not* informing the seller prior to closing.

Buyers can gain leverage on the former owner, especially if the seller financed some of the buyer's purchase. And especially if the purchase and sale agreement include provisions that empower the buyer after closing to revise some of the terms of the agreement.

Buyers and sellers sandbag so they can delay negotiations or a business deal in the hope of receiving a more favorable offer from somebody else or to force concessions in their pending transaction.

"Hiding the ball from each other" is how some people define sandbagging.

Countering sandbagging.

Your first defense against sandbagging is your offense. Wouldn't it be nice if everyone, from the get-go, involved in the evaluation of a company and dealmaking would explicitly request and agree to realistic transparency and fairness?

I don't mean giving up fair-play negotiating advantages!

Among the resources you can access online and from this book, is an article by **Brendan J. McCarthy, Esq.**, *Sandbagging in M&A Deals: Is Silence Golden For Buyers?* Here's an excerpt:

- Imagine this scenario: You have signed a purchase agreement to acquire a business and the parties are now driving to close the deal. The eleventh hour has arrived, and the seller proceeds with a "data dump" of documents that should have been disclosed prior to signing. During your review of the documents provided at this late hour, you learn of the inaccuracy of one of the seller's representations regarding the business. Nevertheless, you believe that any losses sustained by the business as a result of the breach will be minimal and you have come too far to walk away from the deal now. You have an out, but you would prefer to close the deal and then potentially bring a claim against the seller to recover if problems develop. What you are contemplating at the moment is sometimes called "sandbagging."

Below are abbreviated (i.e., incomplete) buy/sell contractual provisions that might help you see how buyers and sellers try to mitigate their risk. (I do not offer legal advice. This book directs you to online resources.)

A buyer-friendly sandbagging provision might look like this abbreviated example. See the entire provision from attorney, **William J. Clements**, in his article, *Buyers and Sellers of Businesses Beware: Due Diligence, Sandbagging and the Destruction of Warranties and Representations.*

- The representations and warranties of the Seller shall not be affected or deemed waived by reason of any investigation made (or not made) by or on behalf of the Buyer . . . knew or should have known that any such representation or warranty is or might be inaccurate or untrue. The Seller hereby acknowledges that, regardless of any investigation . . . and regardless of the results of any such investigation, the Buyer has entered into this transaction in express reliance upon the representations and warranties of the Seller made herein.

Sellers try to exclude the buyer's sandbagging provision. Or sellers may include an anti-sandbagging provision.

Here's an incomplete seller-friendly anti-sandbag-provision:

- To the extent Buyer knew or should have known that any representation and warranty made by the Seller is or might be inaccurate or untrue, Buyer hereby releases and waives any and all claims against the Seller by Buyer arising out of breach of that representation and warranty.

It's up to you to learn more about this topic, and to find advisors that can help you. I am not referring or recommending anyone I mention in this book because I do not know enough about them. I'm merely sharing with you some of my homework.

24 things that can destroy *worthwhile* transactions.

Here are some of the things that can destroy deals that *should* occur.

Poseurs. Poseurs are people who try to impress others by behaving disingenuously. Sellers do it. Buyers do it. And neither are doing anything more than playing a role for fools. I'm talking about presenting false impressions.

Company owners can do it by pretending they are for sale when in fact they're looking for ways to improve their company, which of course too many potential buyers will suggest. And, who wouldn't like free business consulting?

Savvy buyers move on when talking to owners that cannot show a provable and a high motivation to sell their company. ASAP!

As for so-called buyers, almost nothing is better for a company's competitors than to pose as a potential buyer or merger partner; they are seeking secrets for their use.

And, well, you know, most of the self-declared buyers are looki-loos, tire kickers, unqualified and otherwise nogoodniks that waste the time of sellers and the sellers' representatives. One way to spot poseurs posing as buyers is to examine the quality of their advisory team. No advisors, you say? That' a clue.

Buyer's credit report and creditworthiness. It takes a knowledgeable buyer or a savvy acquisition team to position the business buyer for the kinds of financial scrutiny that arises during dealmaking. If and when buyers quit their job to buy a company can have a huge bearing on whether or not a deal can occur. Likewise, how and when the potential buyer manipulates the buyer's finances and borrowing power. And, let's not forget honest asset protection for buyers who don't want everything they own to be on the line.

Remorse. Buyers have it. Sellers have it. You might think we should be thinking about this near the end of this book, because remorse denotes a feeling of guilt and regret that happens after something has happened. Oh no, when it comes to offering companies for sale and buying them, both sides of the deal suffer remorse several times as they progress toward a transaction. And it's normal to occur after closing. Even if the done deal is going to be a win-win worthwhile deal for everyone.

If any member of your potential advisory team cannot explain to you, upfront, before you hire them, how remorse raises its ugly head and how the advisor has helped clients get through it, you might want to keep interviewing advisors.

Value. There are two kinds. The value of the company for sale. And the respective values of the seller and the buyer, either of which are enhanced or diminished by the value of their respective advisory teams.

As to the worth of the company, it's in the eye of the beholder. Incompetent appraisers lead the charge. Naïve clients use unrealistic reports to browbeat the other side of their dealmaking table. This usually makes everyone mad, except for the appraisers smiling on the way to their bank.

As to the sellers and buyers, themselves, the higher the **seller's** motivation to sell, the lower the value of the company, unless the buyer's acquisition team doesn't know how to play that card.

Sellers, of course, want to attract the buyers who can immediately propel the company into more success, which usually means the buyer will pay more for the company. Plus, savvy sellers want to attract kinds of buyers willing to bid against each other. The best business brokers know how to accomplish this for sellers, but if you sellers try really hard you can hire an intermediary who neglects to do this.

Oh, and one more thing to write down: "reasonable range of value." Any request for a selling price below or above that range is probably going to kill the deal. The worst advisors do not know how to compute that range, but their fee to try could be cheap.

Advisors. If you're a potential client, I guarantee that you will have more fun and adventure if you hire people who don't know too much about the kind and size of deal you want to make. Better yet, like holiday dinners with your least favorite family members, it's much more interesting to employ advisors who can't play well with anyone, especially the people on the other side of the dealmaking table. And, there's something else!

Too many deals fall apart because one or both sides of the dealmaking table don't get their stories straight. The time to agree on what's to be said, and by whom, and how to consistently express what needs to be communicated is before a company is offered for sale and before a buyer ventures into the marketplace. What's the point? *Credibility*. Don't compromise it.

Surprise-Surprise! Good for birthdays. Not so much during dealmaking. The best advisory teams show clients how to anticipate and prepare, well before the buyer or seller need to communicate. The best time to craft an explanation for bad news is before disclosing it or before the other side discovers it. Nobody likes playing the fool, so don't play hide-and-seek. This goes for sellers . . . and buyers.

It used to be better! Thou doth protest too much, methinks, is a figure of speech from Hamlet, which can cause doubt about the seller's explanation that the company's horrible performance was an anomaly. Good times are around the corner.

The best way for sellers and buyers to sail this sinking ship is to include on their respective teams so-called turnaround artists who suggest they can turn a sow's ear into a silk purse.

I wouldn't have a drink with you but I'll work with you. Of course, I'm referring to cultural clashes between the potential buyer of the company and its employees (and maybe the suppliers and customers, too).

The best deal killers carefully scrutinize the people. If a white-collar person cannot mix well with blue collars; all sorts of uncomfortable situations arise after the company changes hands.

Negotiating is not for sissies. It is also not for first-timers.

No matter how nicely people behave, negotiating is like making sausage. It's not for the faint of heart; it is messy, sometimes disgusting. If you want to crater a deal, hire a lousy negotiator, which might include yourself. And probably does for buyers and sellers who negotiate directly with each other.

Write this down: Who will wear the black hat when something unpleasant must be said? Do you want to be blamed for it? Wouldn't it be better to blame someone else, such as a member of your advisory team?

Ownership. What's the proof? Such as intellectual property. And what about that machinery over there?

I still shudder when I recall the new owner of a manufacturing company that had been leasing some of its expensive equipment. The buyer assumed, during his plant tour, that everything he saw was owned the company. Oops! (Maybe now you will think about the professionals who specialize in the appraisal of assets.)

Not looking beyond the borders. Yeah, there are beautiful, balmy towns in certain countries south of the good old USA . . . known to kidnap or kill tourists. It's not enough to seek the pretty pictures of the town. You must examine the country.

In business, the least useful advisors put more time into examining the company for sale than evaluating the business' industry. And with the encroachment of the Internet, lots of industries are losing competitive advantages to online product-and-service purveyors.

Records. It's okay to spend lots of time and money trying to decipher the lousy reports and records that sellers foist upon buyers. Of course, exhaustion and frustration quickly overcome buyers. Lucky for them their deal killing advisory team is ready, willing and able to try to make sense out of nonsense. Instead of telling their client to walk away. Right now.

Blue sky. Oops! Did I say "blue sky"? I mean to say "potential." You know . . . how much better the company will become for its new owner.

This is another opportunity for deal killers . . . especially if they don't know enough about what they don't know, which might encourage them to bless what should be a deal shot in the head.

Realizing too late what "the day after" means. I can count on all my fingers and toes the number of disgruntled business buyers who discover during their transition into their acquisition that they should not have bought the business. I can do this count weekly if I look beyond my backyard at the deals closing in the USA and Canada.

The worst advisory teams do not, early enough, focus their potential buyers and sellers on what must be done early in due diligence to anticipate and, hopefully, disarm trouble that can arise after closing.

As for sellers who promise buyers "transition assistance" I am not going to laugh out loud about this. Ask your advisory team about it.

What's not said? Undisclosed actual or potential risks and liabilities, for example. Or the true reason the company is for sale. Of course, you have to know what to look for if you want to find it . . . especially during due diligence.

The worst kinds of deal killers help you move on to the next potential deal. And their billing clock starts over. Yahoo!

The letter of ill-intent. Of course, some deal killers provide their clients with letters of intent to purchase a company that is poised to let the buyer unfairly change the terms of the deal, preferably way down the road, after the seller has invested time, money and hope in the pending transaction.

Naive buyers, unfortunately, fall for this dealmaking ploy only to find out most sellers will tell the buyer to take a hike. And then their advisory team's billing clock starts over.

Lawsuit. Never much fun, and rarely fun in the midst of dealmaking when the company for sale becomes embroiled in litigation. It gets worse if the litigation team wants to milk the company of its value, which makes the business less attractive to buyers.

Yawn! I'll get around to it. The worst teams will let their clients prepare, the night before, for what's coming up.

Tip: Prepare early so you can promptly fulfill requests for information. Delay is offensive; don't expect tolerance; don't ask for it.

Respond quickly; respond adequately. And if you think I am only talking about seller responses, wrong. Buyers can keep the seller's interest and commitment to the deal by requesting information as soon as possible.

And be reasonable. And keep the ball rolling. Momentum is good. Inertia is not.

The company has the licenses and permits. Can the potential buyer qualify for them? If you're looking for a company to buy and you don't know about this, find out now.

My partner or spouse agrees. Really? In some community property states the law requires the spouse to sign off on the sale or purchase of community property.

He said, she said. AKA representations and warranties. AKA misstatements, smoke and mirrors, wishful thinking and "you're on your own after closing; don't call me!"

If deals haven't fallen apart by the time legal counsel argues about the scope and definitions of so-called representations and warranties, now's the time. It's when the best deal killers and deal breakers disrupt their unsuspecting clients.

Extortion. Oh, I know extortion is a strong word. But what else can we call it when people pop up to unfairly force, during dealmaking, the seller or the buyer of a company to provide heretofore unavailable benefits to gain their cooperation for the pending transaction? I'm referring to an acronym I coined: "CELBS," which means customers, employees, landlords, banks (sources of financing) and suppliers. These are the important constituencies.

What's the antidote? Incentives. Forestall speedbumps by anticipating them. Your team should know how to help you craft incentives so CELBS do not obstruct you. Or, at least to minimize their disruption.

What! Taxation? There's a tax on this? Write this down. "Allocation of the purchase price." There's even an IRS form for this (look it up).

Now write this down: "Have all the kinds of taxes that should have been paid been paid?" Such as sales taxes, to name one of several.

It's no fun for the government guy in the wrinkled white shirt to show up to audit the records of your recent business acquisition or merger. So, if this is the kind of fun you seek, be sure to hire an accountant, nee bookkeeper, who doesn't know squat about taxation and, better yet, wait until closing to do so.

Perfect is imperfect! Remember these lyrics from the 1963 Jimmy Soul song, which I've amended for you: "If you want to be happy for the rest of your life, never make a pretty woman / handsome man your wife/husband." And now this reality:

- There are no perfect companies.

- There are no perfect deals.

- Run, don't walk, away from anyone who tells you so.

Chapter 5

Preparing to Buy a Business

This chapter will help you understand the processes and challenges as you plan your purchase of a company.

An ounce of prevention is worth a pound of cure.

You ARE buying a business if you are an employee.

When you're an employee, you ARE buying a business . . . for your employer, though you may not have thought of it that way.

The profit your employer earns on your labor creates value for his business.

What are you left with?

Is it enough to live the lifestyle you want, or to be financially secure when you retire?

Sure, it's risky to buy a business. But it's also risky to be an employee, especially if you're not paid enough to save enough. You can be fired. The company can go out of business if management can't do its job. Right?

If you keep doing for the next 3-years what you've done the last 3-years, where will you be?

Begin on the right foot.

Decide to buy the *right* business the *right* way. Don't look for a turnaround opportunity, a company in trouble. Why? See this topic herein: "Don't buy a loser." Avoiding troubled companies can position you to "buy the *right* business." And then you can acquire it "the *right* way."

What is the *right* business? Part of the answer pertains to the company itself. Another part pertains to you.

The safest, most profitable way to buy the right business is to purchase one that is mature, profitable, having sustainable competitive advantages, and which is not facing insurmountable and material internal or external obstacles or risks. There are ample opportunities for you to find and acquire companies that meet that criterion if you cast a wide net, which accesses the "hidden" market of businesses for sale, and if your approach to sellers is designed to appeal to them rather than repel them. Romancing works better than arguing, especially early in your communications with sellers and their representatives.

- *How to **Prepare** Yourself and **Find** the **Right** Business to **Buy***

- *How to **Buy** the Right Business the Right Way?*

The *Dos, Don'ts & Profit Strategies*, in those books, help you avoid mistakes, make savvier decisions and own a profitable company that compensates you well for managing it, provides a good return *on* your investment during your ownership, and then *returns* your investment plus its growth when you sell your company.

Fueling buyer competition can burn you.

Dumb deals are fueled by buyer competition. The best business brokers create buyer competition, which encourages a bidding war. Baby Boomers hunting for acquisitions are increasing buyer competition. Financial reporters say the greatest transfer of wealth has been and will continue to occur over the next decade; much of it is tied up in family businesses. Too many buyers do dumb deals because they have to outbid the horde of other buyers. You can avoid most of the competing buyers by accessing the hidden market of mature, profitable and fairly priced small and midsize companies that are quietly for sale by-owner. According to one of the most prolific dealmakers, *Arnold S. Goldstein*, whose tell-it-like-it-is books and educational materials have guided people for decades: "Most sellers turn to brokers after all other efforts to sell have failed."

"Most small business deals are made without a go-between."

— *Changing Times*

Your competitive advantage may dissolve once a broker is on scene, but you can have an advantage by being the first buyer to see broker listings.

Procrastination costs you!

Don't unnecessarily let procrastination cost you! You forego the salary and business profit you could earn from owning a company until you consummate a purchase. You waste money fast. If it takes one week from today to get started, and you would earn $10,000 per month from your target business, you "lose" $2,500. A delay in buying can cost you as much as paying too much. It's like standing on the sidelines during a rising real estate or stock market.

Buyer enthusiasm isn't always enough.

Buyer enthusiasm isn't always enough. In fact, it can lead to a fatal case of buyer's fever. We tell buyers to be careful if they act on what they know because, if they are wrong or don't know *everything* they should know about purchasing a business, they can make a BIG mistake.

Consider this story:

A knight returned to his king after a successful campaign. "Your grace," he said, "I have waged war in your name these past months, and conquered many foes. I have led assaults on castle after castle. Their lands and riches are yours. Your enemies in the east have been subdued." The king, having taken the first part of this message with great excitement, suddenly widened his eyes. His jaw dropped. He sputtered, "But I have no enemies in the east!" The knight swallowed, and quietly replied, "You do now."

I hope this story convinces you that enthusiasm isn't always enough. Neither is acting on what you know, because if you are wrong or don't know everything you should know, you can make a BIG mistake.

Buyer fever can kill you.

It is okay, and maybe useful, to catch buyer fever. But, as in love, it's a good idea to know what makes you hot in a good way and what does not.

"Death" from business buyer fever occurs when buyers want a particular business so badly that common sense goes out the window. Even people who know what to do sometimes do the wrong thing, especially if they have a bad case of buyer fever. Don't let buyer fever kill you.

What can cause a fatal case of buyer fever?

Symptoms include:

- Buyer competition, real or phony. It can increase your temperature.

- Deciding upon your acquisition criteria after you commence your search.

- Advisory team infected by conflict-of-interest.

- Inadequate due diligence.

- Being unaware of the selling prices and terms of sale for similar businesses.

- Weak-knee negotiating.

- Too-easily influenced by the seller and seller representatives.

- Using "good luck" business valuation methods.

- Non-definitive purchase and sale agreement.

- Verbal promises, representations or understandings.

- Premature closing.

Business buyers who know how to search for winners don't worry about losing opportunities; worthwhile deals are like buses; more will be by soon.

Art of the deal.

A few years ago, a reporter asked Donald Trump what he was going to do now that he'd lost much of his money. Trump replied:

"Once you learn how to make money, it's no problem getting more."

Some of what "The Donald" knows is in this book. You, however, have to supply the desire and courage.

Collaboration, confrontation, assertion, aggression?

To what degree will collaboration, confrontation, assertion and aggression comprise your communication style with sellers and other people with whom you will interact? Now is a good time to decide; your decision will influence your progress toward buying a business. Will your communications, especially your tone, be more likely to drive the parties toward or away from a done deal? When collaboration is not working, try respectful confrontation. You will get better results if your behavior is consistent.

Ask yourself these questions about financial security.

Can you retire before you die? What will be your standard of living if you quit working? If your net worth and/or passive income cannot support your lifestyle, will it be necessary for you to work until you die? If the possibility of downward mobility is not acceptable, owning a profitable business may be for you.

Understand this about seller financing.

Most sellers won't want to do it.

How and when you propose it makes the difference.

Rely on your acquisition advisor for the communication script and the terms of financing that you'll discuss with sellers and brokers.

There's no a generic communication or contractual terms.

Expect the broker and/or the seller to:

- Check your credit report, review your financial statements and maybe do a background check.

- Seller financing may permit the seller to take back the business in 60 days or less if the buyer defaults on the terms of the loan.

Be careful about the definition of default; it can go way beyond your obligation to make payments when due. Just like bank financing agreements.

An example is your obligation to regularly submit reports to the former owner, such as to prove the company's inventory is maintained at a specific level during term of the loan.

Seller financing usually ranges from 5 to 7 years. Some sellers will accept interest-only payments plus one or more balloon payments of the principal during and at the end of the duration of the loan. The interest rate may be the same rate as institutional lenders. The most motivated sellers will finance more than half of the purchase price.

Is it smart to pay cash for a business?

A better question is this: Is it smart to use *your* money to pay cash for a business?

Probably not. Think about leverage.

Suppose you have $500,000 to buy a business. You could use it to fund a $500,000 purchase price. Or you could use your $500,000 for the down payment on a much larger business.

Wouldn't you rather have the profit from a larger than a smaller company?

And a higher return on your investment, thanks to financial leverage?

Calculate your lost opportunity costs.

According to wikihow.com, "Evaluating a financial decision often means predicting possible costs. If you have a decision to make, choosing one option means a missed opportunity. Looking at the opportunity cost of each choice can help you find the most valuable opportunity." Numerous websites, including wikihow.com, further explain this; some provide a calculator.

You miss out when you don't take advantage of opportunity. *Financial* lost opportunities mean you forego money. You can also forego time and pleasure. It costs you to do nothing, because you defer or forego the benefits you could have enjoyed if you moved forward or if you didn't quit.

Don't proceed without goals.

It is essential that you identify each of the goals you want to achieve with your business purchase. These goals will come in handy as you search for and screen companies. Your goals will be an important guideline during your negotiation to buy the business. Your obvious goal, if you don't already own a business, is to earn income and build your net worth by running your own show. If you already own a business you might want to trade up or trade into another industry. You might want to acquire another business to gain its market share (locally or beyond); to control a better workforce or acquire other assets such as machinery; to get title to intellectual property such as trade secrets, patents, trademarks, copyrights and license agreements; to get a leg up on your competitors by acquiring research and development that you can exploit; to broaden or strengthen your channel of distribution; to qualify to procure larger customers because of your bigger size; to take advantage of economies of scale that increase your profit.

Your experience doesn't have to limit what you can do.

Business owners with fewer than 100 employees, in an *American Express* poll, were asked: "How did you learn your job?" 70% said, "On-the-job experience." Formal education provided a foundation, but the street-smart skills it takes to do the job come from doing the job. These owners looked to mentors, such as the former owner, employees and advisors.

> *One of the characteristics of rich people is that they focus on opportunities, while poor people think of obstacles. Coasting will only get you to one place—the bottom of the hill. Don't let your lack of knowledge become an obstacle.*
>
> — *Ron Sturgeon*

Don't wait for Miss Perfect.

Don't search for or wait for Miss Perfect. You don't have to love it to like it. If you need to own a business, buy a business with a decent future that will provide your immediate income need. That is the most likely way to build enough financial security to support your family in retirement and handle personal financial catastrophes along the way. If the business does not have enough horsepower to accomplish your goal, leverage it into a better one. Time is money. Don't stand on the sidelines for long.

Assess marketplace reality.

The dearth of mature, profitable and fairly-priced small and midsize businesses during and after the Great Recession is throttling dealmaking. Depending upon the industry, there has been as much as an 80% decline of worthwhile sellers the past few years. It's easier and more productive to use a shotgun than a rifle. Too many wannabe buyers have too few targets to hit.

Begin with realistic acquisition criteria.

Criteria include business type, size, age, location, customer and product diversification, degree of competition, working hours, travel requirement, etc. A safe and profitable business acquisition pays the owner a fair salary and benefits, earns enough profit for the business to pay for itself, provides a decent return on investment and later will sell for more than the price you paid.

A few days after buying a business, the new owner went to a fortune teller who looked into a crystal ball and said, "Owning your business will be a living nightmare for the next three years." "Then what will happen?" asked the man hopefully." "Then you'll get used to it"

What size of company fits you?

Large acquisitions are not practical for private party buyers. Small ones are typically an incubator or a dead-end. Medium size businesses (annual revenue ranging from a couple of million dollars to ten million dollars) offer safety and the best return because they are abundant, mature and most likely to qualify for a leveraged buyout, which means your share of the down payment is minimal.

Your criteria relate to what you want to do in business.

Purchasing an established company is one of several ways to get into business. But you don't have to buy a business to be in business. Becoming a licensee is an example. You can acquire from a company the right to manufacture or sell their product. You can outsource manufacturing or sales to another company, which has greater financial resources, production capacity or marketing clout than you do. This tactic can reduce your risk because you won't make the necessary investment in equipment, employees, etc. Your product can be mass-marketed faster. You may earn less profit per unit sold, but you can earn more money because of the increased volume. And someone else copes with the operational headaches.

My company is another example of this. We train people to use our trade secrets, know-how and dealmaking tools so they can start or diversify a professional advisory service. It is mutually beneficial. We earn revenue we otherwise wouldn't get and they don't have to reinvent the wheel regarding the methodologies and content that comprises our consulting niche.

Do it like the "creator" of the Monopoly game did.

Instead of buying the company, buy something from a company owner that you use to build your company.

For example, according to a *New York Times* article, "The Progressive Who Didn't Pass 'Go'", you could emulate Charles Darrow, the "creator" (he wasn't) of Monopoly. Elizabeth Magie created a board game materially similar to Monopoly. Darrow adapted Magie's game and brought it to Parker Brothers, the toy and game manufacturer. Parker Brothers struck a deal with Magie to purchase her patent, and then made millions of dollars. Elizabeth Magie received a pittance in comparison which, when she sold her patent, might have seemed like a good deal to her.

If you already own a company, how about a merger?

Emulate big corporations. Combine with a competitor or a company where your business would complement its organization. Be the acquiring company or be acquired. This is the most common way to substantially and quickly magnify wealth. Most small business owners overlook it.

Grow by mergers and acquisitions.

The safest, fastest, most economical way to grow a small or mid-size business is by mergers and acquisitions. It's also the most profitable growth strategy.

Let's face it. Growing your company by "fighting" your competition is the hard way. Whenever you get a competitive advantage, your competitors copy you. When you "steal" their customers or employees, they do the same to you. When you launch a new marketing program, it takes time and money before you know whether it succeeds or fails. This is business-as-usual for the typical owner.

The street-smart owner uses a better way to grow a company and increase personal net worth: Acquire the competition or another type of business. It's what the "big boys" do. You can do it too with the right guidance.

Expand through business acquisition for these immediate benefits:

- Reduce the quantity of competitors,

- synergism when companies combine,

- penetrate new geographic markets,

- gain inaccessible customers,

- diversify products and services,

- obtain skilled employees,

- update or acquire technology,

- have more purchasing power with suppliers,

- convert your mature business into an emerging one,

- enjoy additional net cash flow from the acquired company, which in turn provides access to more sources of capital.

And the biggest benefit? Bigger businesses sell for a higher multiple of profit. Bigger is better.

So, please remember this: There's an easy way and a hard way to grow a business.

- The hard way: Beat the competition.

- The easy way: Eat the competition.

Example-Merge small businesses for big profit.

Here's a story about mergers among small businesses and the power of economies of scale. It's also a cautionary tale.

It's a little idea with the potential for big opportunity. Especially if you get the timing right.

You might recall the proliferation, in the 1980s and early 1990s, of print shop franchises. They created more print shops than the marketplace could profitably support.

(You're seeing this kind of unhelpful proliferation and industry saturation, today, for other kinds of businesses, aren't you?)

The owner of an independently owned and operated shop hired me. He was nervous because the customer-pie wasn't growing. Worse, the slices were diminishing thanks to new competition generated by the incursion of franchised print shop startups. The owner was thinking about selling his profitable company. I suggested that he postpone selling until we could improve the company's competitive advantages, which would increase the value of the business.

Using a script I prepared and rehearsed with him, the owner asked competing print shops if they were worried about industry saturation. Most were.

So, he bought two of them, each of which served mostly differing market segments within his locale; the kinds of customers he did not serve. Both of the acquisitions were earning a modest profit. Their owners wanted out because they, too, didn't want to cope with what was looking to be profit-weakening industry saturation.

The idea was to operate from one location, so the surviving company (my client's) could be more efficient and profitable.

Before the consolidation these print shops were only running one shift. So, the soon-to-be-larger company shut down the shop with the least desirable location. The employees from the closed shop went to work for the surviving shop. They worked the (new) second shift.

Later, in the next M&A transaction, the acquired company was shut down and its employees were hired for the (new) third shift at the surviving shop. (There was no second or third shift before the consolidation.)

Closing two print shops enabled the surviving company to sell most of the tangible assets that were owned by his former competitors. The proceeds from the sale of equipment and vehicles, plus the elimination of redundant inventory and overhead, created a windfall profit for the surviving print shop.

My client used some of the cash he generated from selling surplus equipment, and the cost savings by elimination of overhead (rent and lots of other expenses), to pay down the financing he incurred to acquire the competitors.

The company immediately increased its profit and improved its competitive advantages. And then the owner sold it for a lot more money than he would have gotten had he sold the company before doing what we did.

You can use this technique to grow your business, even if your industry is not saturated with competitors.

But, think twice before trying to grow by consolidating businesses within a (soon-to-be) suffering industry.

The accomplishments achieved in the printing industry were significantly reduced when desktop computers, printers and software made it easy and cheap for former customers of print shops to design and publish documents. (And with 3D printing, which is coming on strong right now, it won't be long before other kinds of companies lose market share.)

Timing and target selection are key.

The timing is now, especially during troubled times. The easiest-to-hit business targets possess common characteristics:

- Do it now! Studies have shown that the greatest value is grabbed by companies whose acquisitions occur during the first wave of M&A activity. When growth by M&A becomes commonplace, the good candidates will have already been "gobbled up." The law of diminishing returns plagues those who arrive late.

- A light-touch will suffice. Move on if it appears that a heavy hand will be necessary for you to convince a target business that M&A will be mutually beneficial; move on if it will be difficult to integrate the target into your business. When you know how it's done, sourcing M&A targets is quick and easy. Abort reluctant targets; good deals are like buses; another one will come by soon.

- A good company whose management has run out of steam or time. Aging management usually reaches a point of diminishing returns. With attention, aging companies can become increasingly stronger.

- Competitive advantages, which exist in the acquirer and the target that will become stronger in the combined entity than are probable for either individual firm.

- Ability to quickly eliminate unnecessary duplication of overhead and achieve other economies of scale.

- Quick and easy post-acquisition integration of the companies.

Scout the other side . . . for the rest of the story.

One of the best ways to sharpen your street-smarts about business buying is to read books and articles aimed at business sellers. Yes, sellers. You will see the buy/sell playing field from the perspective of company owners and their advisors.

What they write may be particularly insightful; you can use their preconceived notions to present yourself more compellingly to them.

The seller's perspective will be useful to you, too, when you work on your business plan and exit plan.

Complexity shouldn't deter you from buying.

Some people, intimidated by the process of finding and buying businesses, turn away from it. Yes, it is difficult to buy the right business the right way. But it is done every day by knowledgeable people. The only thing (besides guts and money) necessary to achieve a profitable done deal is know-how. You bring to the table your business management capability and maybe your dealmaking experience. Augment yourself with the know-how your buying team brings to the table.

So, you have a financial angel, do you?

Do you have an investor or a pool of investors who you think will provide capital to you so you can purchase a company, perhaps a bigger company than you could purchase using only your money and borrowing power?

- What is your legal and financial structure with investors?

- How much of the money will come from your own funds?

- What percentage of the total capital will that represent?

- Do you now have the other investors' money in your control?

- Do you realize that you can spend months and big bucks putting together a deal, only to have it fall apart at the end because a so-called investor got cold feet? How would that be for you?

If you don't believe that's what can and does happen, ask an attorney who is knowledgeable on buy/sell transactions.

Right now is the time to be getting specific with your investor "angels." Set out roles and responsibilities, and set criteria specifying what constitutes a deal that everybody will go for.

You can do this with a letter of commitment from each of your partners stating the criteria that will induce them to produce a given amount of money within a fixed period. This can get rather involved, just hammering out the criteria and getting everybody to agree. Whatever you do, you should get an attorney to review this before everybody signs off, because it's easy to end up in violation of the securities laws.

Another way to handle this is to set up a corporation where you are all stockholders. Unless you structure it right, you really don't get silent investors that way. You could try a limited partnership where you're the general and the others are limited partners. Either way, you are going to need some good legal advice now rather than later, and it's not going to be cheap. And remember, a good rule of thumb is that the complexity of a deal and the likelihood of it falling apart are equal to the square of the number of players involved.

Thinking about being a "do-it-yourselfer"?

Thanks to the internet and the plethora of how-to publications for buyers and sellers of small and midsize companies, it's easy to glean helpful insight. It's also easy to become misinformed.

No matter how much you learn about buying and selling businesses, if you've not achieved several profitable done deals, you don't know enough. Sure, you have book learning, but you won't have the kinds of experiences and street-smarts that the best advisory team can share with you. So, if you enjoy uncertainty, missteps and spending more time and money than necessary, doing-it-yourself might be for you.

If not . . . consider these reasons for assembling your advisory team:

- They know more than you do; they've been there done that;

- they're on the playing field every day, the longer the better, which means they can access more and better opportunities than you can;

- they've witnessed countless mistakes; they can help you avoid trouble and help you resolve the inevitable disputes that arise during dealmaking;

- they've seen the least and the most creative kinds of dealmaking, which can give you more alternates during the heat of due diligence, valuation and dealmaking;

- because they know the right questions to ask and when to do it, you can avoid stepping on your feet (which is a fast and easy way to repel sellers and their representatives);

- they can better-assess your situation, capability and goals, thanks to their independence and experience.

Being a "do-it-yourselfer" has it place. Such as washing your car. But not so much when buying and selling businesses. Unless you can cope with your dream becoming your living nightmare.

Keep this in mind: You can hire advisors who read books and attend continuing education events. You can hire the people who train professionals and publish how-to information. Think about it.

Assemble your acquisition team before searching.

Buying a business is a team effort. Your advisory team provides you with essential information and connections that you lack. Your team starts with a *Business Buyer Advocate*. Assemble your support team before beginning your search for a business to buy. Do not rely on the seller's or a business broker's advisory team.

Your team also includes an attorney, accountant, appraiser and sources of financing. Each of these members has distinct duties which should not overlap nor compete. You are their manager.

Buyers who do not select the right team of advisors to facilitate a win-win deal may have one or more deal killers. This means you can lose opportunities that wiser buyers enjoy.

You will be at a disadvantage if you talk to sellers or brokers before your team coaches you on how to handle your initial contact as well as the 22-step sequence to safely buy a business.

"Am I going to mind sweeping the floors?" *Forbes*: Two weeks after closing the deal to buy a small medical equipment distributor, the buyer got a disturbing phone call from her bank. The banker wanted to know what she wanted to do with the third account. The third account? The new owner knew about the petty cash account and the corporate checking account, but she didn't know anything about a third account. The third account was the one the business' previous owner had used to manipulate profit. The banker's call was the beginning of a year-long nightmare. This was a case where a buyer thought she had covered all the bases. She hadn't relied upon advisors. She was a DIYer.

Events tend to repeat themselves. The tide of opportunity comes to us all. And when we are prepared for opportunity, our chance is sure to come. Success doesn't depend upon being at the right place at the right time. It depends upon being ready.

— Wynn Davis

Keep specialty advisors in their cage.

You are the decider. Lawyers, accountants and appraisers should advise you, not decide for you; they should not tell you to buy or not buy a business; they should stick to their specialty, which is, respectively, law, accounting and appraisal.

The best acquisition teams include someone whose specialty is business acquisitions and dealmaking. Involve, as necessary, experts in market research and finance.

Here is a tip: Assemble your team, and then call a team meeting that your entire team attends. Do it before you begin your hunt for an acquisition. Discuss your acquisition criteria and your qualifications to achieve the deal you seek. Carefully observe your team members in action. The best time to make changes in the team is before you meet the precious few worthwhile sellers. (One of the most useful roles I and my associates play, when we are the first selection for acquisition advisory teams, is to help our clients assess their team or to refer our clients to the best lawyers, accountants and appraisers known to facilitate worthwhile done deals, people known not to unnecessarily kill deals.)

A man who is his own lawyer has a fool for a client.

Cutting and pasting provisions from legal documents to derive your own is an easy way toward disaster. There simply are too many variables among businesses and dealmaking. Every legal document should be tailored to fit the situation.

Business brokers are not kidding.

Brokers warn about deal killers. We agree. Too many advisors are deal killers, not because a profitable deal can't be done but because the advisors are too risk-averse or don't know how to make a deal happen. Don't feel like you were left at the altar. Establish your acquisition criteria and then use your team to find and make a profitable deal.

Don't let anyone give you rose colored glasses.

Company owners, their employees and everyone else relating to the company see the business from differing perspectives.

The higher the motivation to encourage you to buy the business the more the people, who are influential to the company, will try to custom fit you with rose colored glasses.

Being blind to reality is not good. Seeing a too-good-to-be-true view of the business, through rose colored glasses, provides a false sense of security.

Watch out for excessively cheerful or optimistic people on the other side of the dealmaking table; their view of the company or the deal may not be as good, for you, as it really is. If the company is so great, why are they trying to sell you on it?

Try to be reasonably optimistic; excessive pessimism can sour every deal no matter how good the deal is or could be.

Don't get duped by a red ribbon deal.

If you are an individual (versus a group of professional buyers), buying a business is best done by yourself. Rely on your advisory team for advice; beware of business buying scams.

There are organizations that promise to find you a good business, analyze it, negotiate your deal and then coordinate the closing for you. All you have to do is put up the money and have sufficient experience to manage the business. Sound good? It does if you don't know any better. What is your risk? You might become the proud owner of a don't-wanter business that's been tidied up to sneak it past you (or an appraiser who simply uses computer software to evaluate a company). The cosmetic patches might also fool a lender into financing the transaction, which, of course, is the debt you personally guarantee.

The best deals are the ones you go out and find yourself, preferably with a *Business Buyer Advocate*. Not prepackaged, no-work, no-worry deals all wrapped up in a red ribbon, where all you do is writing a check. These red ribbon deals can tie you up in financial knots.

Remember the Red Ribbon Rule: If a deal sounds too good to be true, it IS too good to be true. If it *is* true, it probably won't be available to you; someone on the inside will seize the opportunity before you hear about it.

Consider all the steps before proceeding.

Don't proceed without considering all the necessary legal and financial steps. Are you going to buy the business in your name or is a partnership or corporation that you control going to buy it? What financial records and capacity will you show, give or *conceal* during dealmaking? What are the tax implications to your decision to own a business? (Income tax and estate tax.) What assets are you willing to convey or pledge to the seller and/or sources of financing? What must you do to comply with existing agreements (e.g., employment, financing) to clear the way for you to buy and operate a business? If you are a business owner, what are you going to do to protect your business from the merger or acquisition that you make?

Readiness to purchase will be a prime indicator of whether they're going to be a worthwhile client to take on, or if they're just window shopping. A primed business buyer is motivated and knows the risk involved with becoming their own boss.

—*United States Small Business Development Center (SBDC).*

Don't buy a job.

Why assume all the risks and headaches of business ownership if you can't earn substantially more than you can from working for someone else? A good business acquisition pays you a salary and benefits at least equal to what the business would pay a manager. Perhaps it also allows you to employ your children or spouse and/ or pass the business along to them when you are ready to retire. In addition, the business' net profit provides a good return on your investment. Anything less is a dumb deal.

Hoping for a performance miracle is just that—hoping.

If your record of accomplishment is mediocre, don't expect sudden improvement, no matter how good the business you buy.

Don't let losing your job cause you to lose your money.

Buying a business can be fun and exciting. It's easy to catch buyer's fever. The antidote for buyer's fever is to run, not walk, away from sellers, brokers, advisors or deals that do not pass your smell test. First impressions are telling; listen to your instincts. To remain in the realm of reasonability, before you abort a potential acquisition, share your concerns with your *Business Buyer Advocate*.

Window-shopping for companies has its place.

Don't devote too much time to this, but window-shopping numerous types and sizes of businesses helps you gain experience and perspective on the buy/sell process. Window-shopping will probably uncover types of businesses you would not have thought about, businesses that provide the features and benefits you seek in a field you did not imagine.

"I'll know it when I see it" wastes time; doesn't work.

If you're unsure, answer this: Would you start a vacation by going to the airport, buying a ticket and getting on the next plane out? Wouldn't you study travel brochures and get opinions from people who have been places? You can learn what they liked and what mistakes they made, so you can plan the best trip possible.

It's wise to know the type and size of business you want because brokers show their best listings to buyers who specify what they want. Brokers and sellers screen out buyers who don't specify the type and size of business wanted as well as the features it should have. If you're not sure of the best business for you, a *Business Buyer Advocate* can help you decide.

Know your actual costs of buying.

Don't neglect to recognize and compute the entire price of a business.

Sure, there is the purchase you pay with money. And then there is your estimate of the potential cash-out-of-pocket you will expend before and after you buy a company. And there are non-financial costs, such as how many more hours you will probably work in the business versus working for someone else, plus the toll on your emotional life as you continually realize the business depends upon you and that you depend upon it. And then, if you did not figure out before buying how you will get out of the company when it is time to exit, you could be committed to the company much longer than you want to be.

Are you willing to pay the entire price?

How to present your financial statement.

Some brokers want you to complete a personal financial statement before meeting with the sellers of businesses. Understand their need to qualify prospective buyers but how much information should you provide at this stage?

Savvy buyers know how to present their personal financial capability.

If you show too much, you increase the probability that you'll pay too much and make a larger than necessary down payment.

If you reveal too little, you won't get a chance to evaluate the company.

Here's my advice, which might change on the basis of a particular client's situation:

- Don't reveal your financial situation without first getting a signed NDA from anyone who will see your financial statement.

- Don't show your entire net worth.

- Don't, upfront, give sellers and brokers your complete financial statement. Disclose all your liabilities and then make sure the amount of your assets, which you disclose, exceeds your liabilities plus the maximum amount of down payment you are willing to make. Maybe add the reasonable amount of working capital you'll inject into the business immediately after purchasing it.

Later, to get their cooperation, you may have to show lenders and the landlord more of your net worth.

If the sum you show is not equal to the seller's expected down payment, tell the seller (assuming you have more money) that you may add more money (don't, yet, explain from where it will come). Or you could tell the seller you intend to use creative financing.

Don't be unnecessarily afraid.

Be prudent. Use common sense. Seek insight and second opinions from your advisory team.

Few people can save their way to financial security.

Americans need a reality check, according to the annual retirement preparedness survey by Merrill Lynch. Most people cannot afford to retire. Despite insufficient net worth or passive income, more than half of people think they will have enough money to retire. Unrealistic thinking has shown up in every Merrill Lynch survey.

If people don't change what they are doing to prepare for retirement, they will have to settle for less.

Why can't you save your way to financial security? First, you work for someone else who gets the profit on your labor. Second, the savings you manage to squeeze out of your overstretched budget are after-tax dollars. This is why it's impossible for 95% of the population to become financially secure.

One reason small business owners do better is they accumulate assets with PRE-tax dollars. When you own a business, you enjoy tax loopholes designed to give you an advantage over the wage earner. And when you sell your company you can arrange for it to continue to pay for your health and life insurance and other benefits in PRE-tax dollars by making it part of your sale agreement with the buyer.

Why shouldn't you make an investment in yourself, which will enrich your lifestyle and your finances, by owning a business?

Getting out of the retirement rut.

The story in *USA TODAY*, "Retirement: Boomers want to keep working - if they can," says many people work well into traditional retirement age. And financial advisers and counselors are encouraging them. Some retirement-age Boomers are working because they have to. They have not saved enough money or they have other concerns.

According to Kelly Greene, a staff reporter for *The Wall Street Journal*, "many people find themselves lost after leaving the office. With so much time suddenly on the horizon, and with so many possible ways to fill it, many retirees find themselves paralyzed by indecision. One way to cut through the clutter is to zero in on your current interests. Sometimes in retirement, you can't change or find solutions to problems on your own. In which case, a coach might help. Don't be afraid to switch gears. The numbers are heard frequently: About two-thirds of baby boomers tell pollsters that they plan to continue working, in some fashion, in retirement."

Your pension may not be secure or enough.

Employer (and governmental) pension plans are changing, and generally for the detriment of employees. It's a false sense of security for employees to think they will receive a pension, or as much of a payout from their pension, as they expect.

"United cleared to ditch pensions," Dave Carpenter, *The Associated Press,* May 11, 2005. "A federal bankruptcy judge approved United Airlines' plan to terminate its employees' pension plans, clearing the way for the largest corporate-pension default in American history."

That court ruling was and is a wakeup call for complacent employees. It has broad implications for people who do not or may not have sufficient net worth to support themselves in retirement.

Buying a business may be the most practical, best shot at financial security.

Don't buy a loser.

According to a Northeastern University study, 80% of businesses in trouble who responded to a survey said they thought they could improve their profitability.

Actual results:

- 55% earned less money after attempting a turnaround.

- 30% continued to operate at the same profit.

- Only 15% increased profit.

If more buyers knew the proven tests to predict profitability, there would not be so many disappointed new owners.

Turnaround specialist Sherwood Partners, which has worked with more than 100 companies, reported a few years ago that for every company the firm has saved, it has overseen the liquidation of roughly three others.

Buy right—you make lots of money and enjoy the lifestyle that business ownership offers! Don't delude yourself about the company's weaknesses. You may not pay much to buy a loser, but you might not get much.

Good luck if you intentionally buy a loser.

Beware of fraudulent conveyance.

A fraudulent conveyance can occur when someone avoids debt by transferring money or other assets to another person or company. Fraudulent conveyance can ensue if the financing of the sale of the business has the effect of depriving the acquired company of the means to pay its debts to general creditors.

- Buyers can lose their investment and the business.

- The seller and creditors may involve the buyer in costly litigation.

- Creditors, including suppliers, become stingy extending credit.

- Business working capital evaporates.

- The business can quickly fail, taking the buyer and seller down with it.

- A violation can exist with a successful business and it might occur even if there is no intent to defraud anyone.

Some accountants and other kinds of advisors refrain from providing a solvency opinion about fraudulent conveyance.

There are various tests of a fraudulent conveyance, which your business acquisition team can explain to you.

Tests include, according to attorneys Katherine A. Gilbert and Kyle J. Wishing, *Due Diligence and Analytical Procedures for Fraudulent Conveyance Opinions*, "(1) the balance sheet test (i.e., a solvency analysis), (2) the cash flow test, and (3) the capital adequacy test."

Company liquidations are more common than sales.

Company liquidations are more common than business sales because sellers:

- Don't know how to find buyers

- Have unrealistic expectations of buyers

- Ask too-high a price for the business

- Expect too-high a down payment

- Are not willing to finance some of the buyer's purchase price

- Expect the buyer to retire too quickly the installment note to the seller

- Don't know how to communicate/negotiate on the subject of selling

- Are too cheap or naive to employ specialized experts in business sales

- Expect too much collateral from the buyer (in addition to pledging the company)

- Don't have enough time to sell before a personal catastrophic event overcomes them. Such an event can inhibit an owner's ability to manage the company (i.e., health disability) or to continue to own it (i.e., death, divorce, partnership dispute).

Don't be a bottom feeder.

Think fish. You know what bottom feeders eat. Yuk! Buying a lousy business because its price is "cheap" may turn out to be false savings. Buy a winner, on street-smart terms, or keep your job or get a job.

Don't be naïve or appear to be naïve.

Sellers and lenders shy away from "buyers" who don't have a clue. To get to second base with sellers, at first base show your managerial and financial capability.

Study our creative financing book (How to Get ALL the Money You Want For Your Business Without Stealing It ™) and you won't have to use as much of your money or personal borrowing power to buy and operate the business.

Don't show and tell too much too soon.

Don't show and tell too much, especially before you know the full agenda of people. Upfront, show sellers and brokers your resume and financial capability. But don't elaborate upon your history, goals, values, etc. Make sure suspicious characters realize that you are not a vulnerable, inexperienced business buyer. Let them know that a "mother ship" (your advisory team) stands behind you.

Being a lone wolf is good for wolves, not for you.

Let sellers, brokers and sources of financing know you have assembled a qualified business acquisition advisory team. It shows them you are sensible and it cautions them against trying to fool you.

Don't buy on the Greater Fool Theory.

The *Greater Fool Theory* suggests it is possible to make money by buying overvalued businesses because there will always be someone else (a greater fool) who is willing to purchase it from you at an even higher price. Another definition is that a greater fool will be your bail out if you buy a lousy business or make the wrong deal on a good business. The *AOL* purchase of *Time Warner* shows the downside of the *Greater Fool Theory*.

Don't buy if you're not qualified to buy and manage.

Before buying, think twice about whether you are qualified to fix or manage the particular company that interests you. Too many buyers, whose pending deal looked good on paper, are shocked to discover after buying the company that they have a tiger by the tail, that they don't have enough business IQ to avoid being mauled. If this is your situation, immediately hire professional advisors. Don't think so? Good luck.

But let's expand our thinking because there are two issues here. Hiring the right business acquisition team is the antidote if you don't know enough about the process of purchasing a company. The other issue pertains to what you know about managing any kind of company. Capable business managers can more effectively transition into their business acquisition.

And keep this in mind: Most people who set out to buy a business acquire one that differs from what they thought they were going to buy. Most buyers have tunnel vision when they begin looking for companies for sale. It doesn't take long for business brokers and the buyers' acquisition advisory team to reveal other kinds of suitable companies. This is a good thing because more potential targets decrease the time to a done deal and increases the opportunity.

Caveat: It is riskier to buy a business outside your business experience (i.e., you're from manufacturing but you want to own a retailer). The more you venture outside your experience, the more important becomes your advisory team, before and after your acquisition, and the more important are the qualifications of the company's employees and the exiting owner's assistance to you as you transition into the company.

Sufficient competitive advantage?

Due diligence is complicated, time consuming and high pressure. It takes organization and persistence. There are generic topics that apply to every kind and size of business.

Here's one example:

Ask this: What are the specific elements of your company's competitive advantage, and how, specifically, do they pay off for you in the marketplace?

Competitive advantage, along with profitability, are the most important factors. Too often people overlook or misunderstand its value. Hearing the seller talk about competitive advantage illuminates a company's vulnerabilities and opportunities.

Savvy buyers and their advisors shy away from sellers that cannot explicitly answer the question, and then prove their answer.

This topic reminds me of the adage: You can put lipstick on a pig but it is still a pig. Don't fall for superficial answers or the promise of recent cosmetic changes to the company. Watch out for sellers who attempt to disguise the true nature of their company and its marketplace.

Competitive advantage exists when a company's profit and reputation is above the norm for its industry. It occurs when the company is more capable than its competitors at managing the resources available to it, such as a superior product with outstanding value proposition.

Remember what Warren Buffett says: The most important thing he looks for when evaluating a company is its "sustainable competitive advantage."

You can derive your own due diligence questions on the basis of your research. And if it doesn't work for you, hire an experienced advisor.

What won't work is to pester sellers and brokers with irrelevant questions, or poorly crafted questions and requests. They won't put up with it.

Buy a business showing sustainable advantages.

Your investment can be safer and more profitable if the company you buy has sustainable competitive advantages. You can forego this warning if you know how to create sustainable competitive advantages, the keyword being "sustainable." Too often people who start or buy companies establish competitive advantages that turn out to be temporary when competitors emulate or surpass them or when the marketplace changes, so what were competitive advantages turn into yesterday's ideas.

Don't buy on a bubble.

A bubble occurs when customers put so much temporary demand on a product or service that the purveyor of the product/service enjoys an extraordinary increase in revenue. If the higher revenue is not sustainable, a bubble occurs. Like soap bubbles, purchasing a business whose value is inflated because of a financial bubble ignores the fact that bubbles eventually pop. Examples abound in many industries. Three of the most obvious are the dot-com bust, diet plan failures and exercise and supplement fads. Children's toys and home improvement or cleaning products provide other examples.

Eager customers rush to the newest cure for their problem and then abandon it to rush to what is touted as an even better (and easier) solution. When this occurs and you are holding the bag (i.e., the business you bought), you might attempt to minimize your loss. One way to do so is to quickly sell your business. If similar businesses are suffering because the bubble burst, a crash in value may occur due to panic selling by owners who want to unload their declining business onto others. You can avoid this by not following the crowd or by answering this question: At what phase in the boom cycle is this opportunity?

The following examples illustrate these topics: reliance upon a single product, fickle customer buying fad, marketplace saturation, franchisor competition with franchisees, penalties for business buyers and owners.

The Washington Post: "McDonald's first money-losing quarter due to sagging sales, aggressive rivals. Sales at McDonald's restaurants dropped 1.6% in the first two months of the quarter. December sales are expected to drop even lower. Meantime, the company continued to open stores despite a slip in sales. Chief Executive Jack Greenberg resigned."

"Carb culture affects stock prices—low-carbohydrate dieters shift food firms' prospects," Kristen Gerencher, CBS.MarketWatch. com: As consumers shift their diets toward more protein and fewer carbohydrates, many food producers are feeling the heat—good and bad—in profits and stock prices. Doughnut-maker Krispy Kreme, pasta giant American Italian Pasta Company and Interstate Bakeries claim to have suffered sales losses. Bakeries, pizza chains and pasta makers are losing sales while companies catering to meat and dairy lovers are gaining because low-carb diets sanction those foods. Krispy Kreme warned that profits would be lower and blamed changing eating habits for reducing its fiscal 2005 forecast by 10 percent. The company also plans to sell or close Montana Mills Bread Company after buying it last year, along with six of its less profitable stores. Shares of Krispy Kreme plummeted 29 percent to close at $22.51 Friday. (Krispy Kreme was selling for nearly $50/share in 2003.)

"Carbs just one hole in Krispy sales," Paul Nowell, *The Associated Press*. Competition from competing retailers of donuts (e.g.., Dunkin' Donuts) and grocery store sales also are cited for Krispy Kreme lag. Dunkin' Donuts' poses a competitive threat because it sells a more diverse line of breakfast foods than Krispy Kreme (which primarily relies upon doughnut sales). J.P. Morgan analyst John Ivankoe cited "waning fad appeal" as one of the company's problems. Krispy Kreme's increased reliance on sales in grocery stores and other retail outlets, which makes the doughnuts more available and therefore less unique, also is hurting business, he said. John Glass of CIBC

World Markets says rapid store expansion and the low productivity of its new stores is having an impact, too.

"Investors sue Krispy Kreme," *Palm Beach Post wire service*. Investors suing Krispy Kreme allege the firm did not tell investors earlier that the low-carb craze was hurting its sales. Krispy Kreme said that the allegations are completely without merit.

"Krispy Kreme's quarter more hole than doughnut," Paul Nowell, *The Associated Press*. Is the glaze permanently off the once high-flying company? Krispy Kreme lost $3 million in its third quarter and an intensifying accounting investigation continues. The SEC is looking into its franchise re-acquisitions. Since May, Krispy Kreme has closed some stores.

Upon reading in 2003 about the premium-priced doughnuts from Krispy Kreme and the firm's intent to franchise its concept, I said: "It's just a doughnut. When the novelty wears out for customers, they will buy their doughnuts from the nearest, least expensive competitor."

Krispy Kreme is an example for other *Business Buying Don'ts*, such as "Don't depend upon one product to sustain the company; Don't forget the most important question—What is the competitive advantage of this company and what are the dependable drivers that create customer demand for its product?"

"Tech Investors Create a Billion-Dollar-Baby Boom," by Michael J. de la Merced and Mike Isaac, cnbc.com, February. 19, 2015, write: Giant sums of money and sky-high valuations are nothing new in the technology industry. But the latest burst of activity has put on clear display the frenzied pace of investors, who are eager to catch the next blockbuster company. The action is also again spurring talk that overeager investors are poised to relive the dot-com boom and bust at the turn of the century, when overinflated start-ups led to a quick and painful downturn. For some, I think it will end badly."

Don't put the cart before the horse.

Establish rapport with sellers so they are thinking: "I like this person; he/she could run my business." And then ask the seller to tell you the secrets about the business. Respect confidentiality.

Don't buy unverifiable "potential."

Just because a business has been profitable is not enough reason to buy it. Relying too much on historical performance is like looking into a rearview mirror to see what is ahead. Buy an independent, mature, profitable business with a good future if you want to win bigger. You make money from DAY ONE.

Too often paying for potential (profit) is praying for good luck. It usually does not pay to buy a loser "with potential."

Don't be duped by window-dressing.

Some sellers are better at spinning a tale about their business than they are at managing it. Sure, the cosmetics are important. But look past the makeup and the seller's claims so you invest in the reality of a business' history, capability and future.

Don't be raring to go with "business opportunities."

With respect to business opportunities (which include some franchises), heed the lessons in the *USA Today* article, "Dreams of riches lost to scams." The article reveals various business startup schemes that are sold by slick talking salesmen who brandish professional looking materials. Middleclass Americans are the perfect target. Most scams promise big money for a small investment.

Stuart Meyer of Northwestern University says, "Panic entrepreneurship describes what happens to middle managers whose jobs have been eliminated. These outplaced executives are ripe birds for the plucking."

The Virtual Concierge was a kiosk at which people could make purchases and reservations, order food and buy tickets. Nearly 26,000 of the machines, with a purported income stream from advertising, were sold to more than 1,800 people. But in reality, fewer than 100 were in operation at hotels, airports and stadiums, the receiver found. The U.S. Securities and Exchange Commission announced fraud charges and an asset freeze, pegging the amount paid by investors at $40 million-plus. The U.S. Attorney's Office filed criminal charges and placed the investment amount at more than $70 million.

On the other hand, unless you like the idea of reinventing the wheel, there is value in paying a legitimate business opportunity seller who invents or improves a business concept, which provides training and tools, which help you to open and manage your business and who offers continuing assistance.

Caveats: Tapping into a going-concern (the seller's system and knowledge) can be good for you, but determine this: Is the organization capable of managing a growing chain of affiliates? New franchises and business opportunities are riskier than other startup businesses.

"Investing" in pyramid schemes is foolish.

If it's too good to be true, it is not true.

Avoid plans that offer commissions to recruit new distributors. Beware of plans that ask you to spend money on costly inventory. Be suspicious of claims that you will make money by recruiting new members instead of selling the product yourself. Beware of promises about high profit or claims about "miracle" products.

Be cautious about references; they could be shills who are paid by the promoter.

Don't pay money or sign contracts in a high-pressure situation. Check pyramid schemes and multilevel marketing plans with the Better Business Bureau and state Attorney General.

Don't be a follower.

Don't buy merely because your friend or relative bought the same type of business. What works for them may not be best for you. Be careful of the comparison game: You feel as though they are getting ahead and you are not; you must be doing something wrong if you don't get into the same business; they know best.

"Every time a friend succeeds, I die a little inside."

— Rohit Khare.

Don't prematurely quit your job.

If you know you will purchase a business, quitting your job too soon may burn desirable bridges with your employer (which could be your safe haven if you fail to acquire a business).

Being unemployed will adversely affect your ability to borrow money for your acquisition. If you are unemployed, self-employment (such as consulting until you buy a company) may be necessary for your survival.

Don't think you won't sacrifice.

The grass is not always greener on the other side. Some people think they will enjoy self-employment more than being a wage slave. Some people are eager to exchange a job they hate for business ownership that they think will be less troublesome.

Life's a struggle and then you die, whether you are an employee or employer. Buy a business because you want the financial rewards and the control that ownership provides.

Pay attention to your family.

Trouble at home frequently leads to business problems. It is easier to pilot your business when the rest of your life is in order. Isn't your responsibility to build financial security for your family? Your business can contribute three ways: Maximization of profit; provision of a succession plan to handle your exit; taking advantage of tax loopholes.

Don't do this, but wish for it.

The best criteria, which was the most unrealistic we ever read was this in the October 1991 issue of *Inc. Magazine*:

"I want a seller who's 75 years old. I want him to have children who are artists and doctors and lawyers and who have no interest in the business. I want a guy who has no idea what his business is really worth and who doesn't even know what a business broker or investment banker is. If he does know any, I want him to hate them. And I want to walk in there and get him to tell me about his business, take me to lunch, and bring me home to meet his wife. I want someone who's selling something more important to him than his wife, his children, and his home. This isn't his business; this is his baby. He created it. And I want him to look at me and say, 'I want you to own my business.' Because once you've made this connection, money is no longer the most important thing to him. He's not going to turn around in the middle of negotiations and sell his baby for a better price to some jerk. "

[Ah, don't we wish?]

When doing nothing can be good for you.

If you have good reasons to sit on the sideline, do so. When the media scoffed at Warren Buffett for not dumping some of his holdings and for not using some of his company's cash to make more investments he replied: "It's a painful condition to be in—but not as painful as doing something stupid." Buffett is known for his patience. He will hold investments that are losing value on paper, only to see them become reinvigorated; he will let pass what "experts" claim to be a hot investment of the week. Maybe that is why he increased Berkshire's book value by an average of 22% per year for four decades.

Don't make major purchases while looking for a business.

You might need the cash and borrowing power to make the best business acquisition. Forego buying a home, vehicle or anything that is expensive.

Don't waste time on slowpokes.

Although it is important to let the seller know you want to buy his business, tactfully cause him to understand your interest is based upon his continued cooperation and the representations he has made about his company (such as it earns the money you want and is not about to be blindsided by its competition or employees). You do not have to say it in words; your attitude can be: "This isn't the only fish in the sea, but it's the one I'm trying for first." Always have more than one deal in analysis so a seller can't slow you down while he gathers and presents the information you require.

Just because a seller says he wants to sell doesn't mean that he will or can do the work necessary to sell his business. Pitch in if you truly like a particular business for sale by a reluctant seller. Ask the seller how you and his team can work together to gather the information you want to analyze.

It's a matter of balance. Unnecessarily waiting is not an acceptable decision. Waiting is for people who don't have other alternatives.

Don't put all your eggs in one basket.

Many handshake agreements between buyers and sellers never come to fruition. Keep several deals in the works (using nonbinding letters of intent) so when a deal falls through you don't have to invest more time, effort and money to go back to square one.

What about non-financial seller omissions?

It is important for buyers to protect themselves from seller omissions that don't have a direct financial impact, but affect operational management of the business (in other words, the company is not as described by the seller)?

Your financial evaluation is not enough to detect the business' vulnerabilities and opportunities.

Ask questions and conduct research into the company about the operation of the business.

Go way beyond the owner and manager. Find out what employees, customers and suppliers have to say.

Make sure your purchase and sale agreement fully address the scope and content of seller representations and warranties.

Don't rely upon a handshake.

Sad to say in this day and age, given the increasingly dishonest practices we see among politicians, businesses, financiers and others, handshakes are for greetings and congratulations; they are not for dealmaking. Get everything in writing, and make it binding, using "subject to" provisions, as necessary, in contracts.

Have a realistic expectation of income.

What you want a business to pay you or what you think is the profit it can earn may not be achievable. Every business in every industry operates within industry parameters. Check the statistics for every type of business that interests you to know what you can expect. You will read comparative standards for most of the elements of income and expense and the relationship between assets and liabilities. This insider information will put into context the relative position of the business you want to buy with respect to its competition.

The worst of times can be the best of times.

Wonderful business buying opportunities abound. Taking the low hanging fruit is as easy as it gets. Accessing the hidden market of the best businesses for sale (preferably before they are for sale) and then using an M&A strategy for growth puts the control in the hands of the principals instead of the moneybags.

Opportunity for Companies

Challenge: Confidence in the economy is worrying owners of small and midsize businesses; some wonder whether it's time to get out, i.e., liquefy (not liquidate) their investment in their company. Or perhaps the personal problems of the owners of small and midsize companies adversely (or are about to) affect their mature, profitable company; this can occur because these companies don't have the depth of management to handle the business when the owner is personally overcome. (Too bad the owner did not employ an M&A strategy to grow the company to achieve a sufficient depth of management.)

Opportunity: Small and midsize companies that are hampered, or are about to be hampered, by the owner's personal situation can create wonderful buying opportunities for those who want to own and manage a business, and for companies that want to grow via an M&A strategy.

Challenge: Rising unemployment.

Opportunity: Most jobless people seek another job. Many have to settle for less. This presents a wonderful window of hiring opportunity for your company to replace deadbeats with great employees.

Challenge: Lenders are limiting, reducing or calling lines of credit (LOC). It's becoming increasingly difficult to switch to another lender, and when it is possible the terms are a bitter pill to swallow.

Opportunity: Show suppliers and vendors why it is in their self-interest to concede better terms so your company can afford to continue to place orders.

Challenge: Falling liquidity levels. It's becoming more difficult to match cash receipts with disbursements; managing day-to-day cash flow will probably get much harder before it gets easier.

Opportunity: If you still have a line of credit, draw as much of it as you can, right now. Put the money in an institution that does not control your LOC. The cost of warehousing "excess" cash can be less than the loss, and lost opportunity, you will suffer if your lender freezes your line of credit and grabs money from your bank account.

Have a "garage sale." Eliminate your least productive employees; reassign their work to your most productive employees whom you can pay a performance bonus using the money you've been wasting on the deadbeats. Sell your unnecessary or the least productive assets. Is it necessary for you to own so many assets? Couldn't you lease instead of owning some of them? Make your suppliers more responsive so you can reduce your inventory levels.

Challenge: Money is tight. Pigs will fly before third-party acquisition financing for small and midsize companies becomes readily available (except to the most astute business buyers).

Opportunity: Acquisitions generally require cash (at least for a down payment), but one of the best kept secrets is mergers can be achieved without much, if any, cash. The fact that no or little cash is necessary to consummate a merger can compel the owner of a mature, profitable company to employ M&A to leapfrog less enlightened entrepreneurs. And, when done right, the post-merger company can be (almost instantly) more profitable. The resulting company can be more formidable than either company would be had they not merged. Don't leap to a wrong conclusion: It is not necessary to grow by acquiring weaklings. Strong can attract strong when both parties know the rules of the game.

Challenge: Concern about asset and investment values, including the price to acquire a small or midsize business. Appraisers and acquirers are sharpening their pencils.

Opportunity: Selling prices of the most desirable small or mid-size businesses won't decline for savvy sellers. Terms of purchase will be as good as they get for the savviest acquirers. Fewer sellers will be able to sell for more than "fair market value." (This assumes that fewer uninformed buyers will try to outbid each other, which may occur if the uncertain marketplace temporarily scares away the amateurs.) What's the fastest route from being an amateur to a pro? Hire a buy/sell expert who has connections and know-how to navigate the *hidden market* in any sort of economic cycle.

Opportunity for Individuals

Challenge: Working for others has been financially rewarding, but you're sick and tired of the politics, the burnout, the uncertainty (you can be fired or things can go from good to bad when you least expect or can afford it); you're making a good living, but you're not making a difference.

Opportunity: If you've been successful (especially in business), you can rejuvenate your worklife and dramatically increase your income and financial security. Simply buy the right business the right way, and then leverage your acquisition into a series of M&A transactions until you have more than you need. You can control your income and how you make a difference when you establish your business acquisition criteria and then implement your growth strategy.

Challenge: You're employed or unemployed; you're concerned about the meltdown of pension and healthcare benefits; you realize your further employment won't create the net worth you require for financial security or a worthwhile retirement; you envy the owners of small and midsize businesses who control their worklife and their income.

Opportunity: If you have sufficient capital for a down payment to acquire a mature, profitable fairly priced business, do it now. Potential deals abound if you know how to find them and if you know how to do the deal. A challenging economy makes it easier; the aging population of business owners makes it easy; and, the three Ds are always in place: death, disability and divorce - these bring to market mature, profitable fairly priced businesses, which must be quickly sold.

Challenge: You're retired or about to be retired, and you don't have sufficient financial resources to adequately fund your retirement. Should entrepreneurship be your next career?

Opportunity: It's usually cheaper, faster, safer and more profitable to buy a mature, profitable company than it is to start a business. But don't jump into the fire from the frying pan.

It's not smart to buy a business unless you have the skills and an advisory team to help you buy the right business the right way.

Think twice about going into business if salesmanship is outside your area of experience. Owners of small and midsize businesses must be adept at marketing and sales; it's fool's gold to believe you can fully delegate these functions.

Challenge: Downsizing creates a horde of unemployed, inexperienced buyers; they create a *seller's* market.

Opportunity: Most of the mature, profitable fairly priced businesses for sale are on the *hidden* market. They don't advertise nor does a business broker or intermediary represent them.

Why settle for some of the businesses for sale if you can access all of them? The *Business Buyer Advocates* at *"Partner" On-Call Network* are deeply connected to the *hidden* market of sellers, including businesses not for sale, but available to the right buyer.

What you can do goes beyond what you know.

"Why some people are richer than others," Robert Kiyosaki, *Rich Dad Poor Dad*, explains why some people succeed in business and others merely dream about it or fail.

"Have you ever had smart students with great grades go out into the world and not do well financially or professionally?" The professor nodded. "When it comes to money," I replied, "it is the emotion of fear that keeps most people poor. Most people live in fear of losing money or risking money so they say things like 'play it safe' or 'don't take risks.'" The professor immediately interjected, "Are you saying to be careless? Live dangerously?" "No," I replied. "All I am saying is that you need to know when you are thinking emotionally and when you are thinking rationally. When you are emotional, thinking rationally is often the hardest thing to do. Money, sex, religion and politics are emotional subjects. So, when it comes to those subjects, most people are not thinking rationally. When it comes to money most people are so afraid of losing that they wind up losing. That is not too intelligent." How you respond to fear makes the difference.

"What is the primary difference between successful people and unsuccessful people?" asked the professor. I nodded my head. "When it comes to money, I am often going in when most people are getting out. Or I take risks, while the masses are playing it safe. "I feel the same fears they do; I just use my mind differently. That ability to do what is necessary, in spite of my feelings screaming at me to do otherwise, is the single most important life skill I have learned." "But aren't you afraid?" asked the professor. "Yes." I replied strongly. "I have the same fear as everyone else. It's how we respond to that fear that makes the difference. As I said, most people would have pulled back on the stick when the engine died, and l was trained to push the nose forward. "The same thing happens financially. People pull back, play it safe, terrified of making a mistake while life's opportunities pass them by."

Assess your risk tolerance.

Can you financially and emotionally handle the problems that might arise? What if your acquisition does not live up to your expectations? Don't let your imagination scare you away from buying a good business. Your *Business Buyer Advocate* can help you identify reasonable possibilities.

Computing your business-buying risk.

Assume that you discover, after purchasing or merging a business, that you bought the *wrong* business or bought the *right* business the *wrong* way.

Your advisory team can help you more accurately evaluate your risks.

Nonfinancial risk. What would be the adverse effect on your time, health, marriage, self-esteem, employment and credit rating if the business fails or if you cannot sell it for what you paid?

Financial risk. Put a realistic price tag on each of these elements of risk. Assume you can't recoup your investment if you sell the company. Calculate it again assuming you must liquidate your bad investment.

- Amount by which you might overpay

- Down payment from your funds

- Personal guarantee acquisition debt

- Interest until acquisition debt paid

- Personal guarantee: business trade credit

- Personal guarantee: business lease

- Accounting fee: Tax opinion & verifications

- Legal fee: Purchase agreement, lease, dispute, etc.

- Commission to seller's business broker

- Lost income while searching for business

- Business less profitable than you thought

- Your added capital needed after purchase

- Surprises caused by poor due diligence

You reduce your risk if you buy a proven winner and if you properly employ the ideas in this book.

Flying blind can kill you.

If you don't know where you want to go and how you are going to get there and especially why you want to do so, you can waste time and money, and maybe not buy the right business the right way. So, talk to your influential others, and your advisors. Ask them to play devil's advocate, to challenge what you say you want to accomplish. And then devise your plan and stick to it. Don't forget to think about your exit plan for the business before you buy it. Be flexible, which means the best laid plans should be subject to change as you progress, for good reasons. What good is there for you if you cannot profitably sell your business when you want to move on?

Know why and when to count yourself out.

Preferably before, but definitely shortly after you buy a business, know who will replace you if you get hit by a bus. Who will step in if you are temporarily disabled? Who will run the show if you are dead? And guess what? Knowing the talent is there when you need it means you can take vacations, leaving in good hands the routine operation of your company. There's more! Someday, when you want to sell out, these people are in-place as your buyer(s) or you can brandish them as your management team to other buyers who want to know your business can thrive without you.

How big (and valuable) is your to-do list?

You work from a to-do list, don't you? (The topics in this book comprise another to-do list!)

Don't underestimate the value and the costs of to-do lists. They should help you, not bog you down.

The co-founder, Mike Lee, of the app, *MyFitnessPal,* in an interview appearing on techcrunch.com, said that he and his co-founder/brother Albert Lee have always had "a thousand item to-do list, and we could only do three things on it." Over time, he said, "things kept dropping off the list, which kept getting bigger and bigger."

Masterminds belong on your team.

Besides your *Business Buyer Advocate*, identify an advisory board that will mentor you *after* you buy a business. Your board can include family members or friends. Select people who bring skills or contacts to the table that go beyond your capability. Wouldn't you like people to bounce ideas off, from whom to get objective opinions?

Don't cheapen your ethics.

What goes around comes around. Be honest (without being naïve). Don't mislead sellers, brokers or your advisory team. Tell it like it is, tactfully.

You can afford to be honest because you can play by the golden rule: you have the gold (money), so you make the rules. This works fine with legitimate sellers so long as you are reasonable.

Word gets around fast when you don't play fairly. For example, the seller or broker you abuse will tell other business owners that there is a renegade business buyer on the loose–you!

Business Buyer Advocates can save a great deal of grief.

Scenario: A business buyer discovers, after purchasing a business, that he bought the wrong business or bought the right business the wrong way. Maybe he is in over his head and can't really manage the company as he thought he could. He regrets his purchase. So, what does he do?

If he shares his grief with a lawyer, the lawyer will probably advise him to look for ways to rescind the transaction. How? By looking for someone to blame for the buyer's mistake—someone like the seller or the seller's advisors. A business broker, for example, makes a very good victim.

So, the buyer and his attorney go over every document that the seller and broker produced or should have produced.

If the seller or broker failed to disclose a material fact, the attorney suggests filing a claim of misrepresentation, fraud, unfair business practices, etc.

If the buyer can't prove his claim, so what? It doesn't cost much to file a lawsuit, and a negotiated settlement is usually possible.

The buyer, actually, may have nothing to lose by pointing a finger at the seller or broker. After all, the buyer has the seller's cash machine, you know—the business—to pay for his attack on the seller or broker.

The brokers I work with say this scenario is all too common.

If you are a buyer advisor, such as an attorney or accountant, don't relax. A buyer tosses a wide net when he's looking for someone to blame. Perhaps this is why street-smart lawyers and accountants stick to their special expertise—legal, historical financial records and taxation.

When it comes to buy/sell transactions, few advisors have sufficient experience and expertise. Prudent ones refer their client to a *Business Buyer Advocate* who specializes in issues that concern business viability, potential, valuation and dealmaking.

An independent *Business Buyer Advocate* enables the seller's broker and advisors to avoid dual agency (trying to serve both sides of a buy/sell transaction).

A buyer may not have as strong a claim of misrepresentation against a seller or business broker if the buyer does not have his own independent business acquisition advisor.

Who else benefits from *Business Buyer Advocates?*

Buyers, sellers, brokers, advisors, appraisers and sources of financing can benefit from *Business Buyer Advocates.*

Buyers: *Business Buyer Advocates* do not divert buyers away from brokers. They advise buyers to include by-owner sellers in the search because this expands the buyers' choices to *all* the businesses for sale. A competent *Business Buyer Advocate* does not disrupt deals; asks reasonable questions; does not under-value a business but will base a business valuation on reality.

Sellers, because a sale occurs.

Business brokers, advisors and appraisers, because a buyer who understands the buying process can expedite due diligence and dealmaking.

Sources of financing, because they can fund better deals.

Keep in mind:

- **A *Business Buyer Advocate*'s mission** is to get the buyer the best value on the most lucrative terms.

- **A business <u>broker's</u> mission** is to get the seller the highest price on the most lucrative terms.

Yes-but—what?

You are a yes-but if you say: "Yes, I want to do it, but (here's my excuse)."

Yes-buts play the loser's game. You are a yes-but if you reject useful ideas you or anyone else generates. You are a yes-but if you say: "I have to get other parts of my life squared away first."

If you really want something, when is the best time to start? The world is full of people who take their dreams to their grave because they plan to start tomorrow. Tomorrow never comes.

Other people might try to tell you that what I'm saying will not work. That is because they do not know what I KNOW.

- They do not know *The Street-Smart Way to Buy a Business* *.

- They do not know the street-smart way to get cash out of a business.

- They do not know the street-smart way to increase business cash flow.

That is why they are skeptical.

Here's what works:

Start by setting a target date; it is the antidote to both procrastination ("Oh, I'll get to it someday.") and despair ("I'll never get there."). The sooner you start getting some of what you really want, the more confidence and energy you will have for the rest of it!

It is not the critic who counts, not the one who points out how the strong man stumbled or how the doer of deeds might have done them better. The credit belongs to the man who is actually in the arena; whose face is marred with sweat and dust and blood; who strives valiantly; who errs and comes short again and again; who knows the great enthusiasms, the great devotions and spends himself in a worthy cause and who, if he fails, at least fails while bearing greatly so that his place will never be with those cold and timid souls who know neither victory nor defeat.

— Teddy Roosevelt

Any business acquisition is feasible if you creatively finance it.

You must know how to talk to sellers, brokers, suppliers, bankers and investors.

If you talk to them without being prepared to answer certain questions about the company you want to buy and the financing you propose, they are going to look at you like you are an amateur, and ignore you!

Guess what? KNOWING creative finance is not enough.

You must FIND a motivated seller before anyone else, and KNOW how to quickly evaluate the company, KNOW what to pay for it, and how to present an offer that will be accepted.

It will not matter if you know how to put together a winner deal if you do not know how to FIND a worthwhile company for sale.

Keep reading this book for more facts, tips and strategies. And then take action!

Chapter 6

Searching for Winners

The first step to buying a company is finding one you want to buy. This chapter shows how to do it, so you can avoid pitfalls along the way.

Searching in the public market is like rowing a boat with one oar; it takes a lot of effort and you don't get far.

Learn how to access the unadvertised and huge hidden market of sellers, which is where to find the best companies and the best deals.

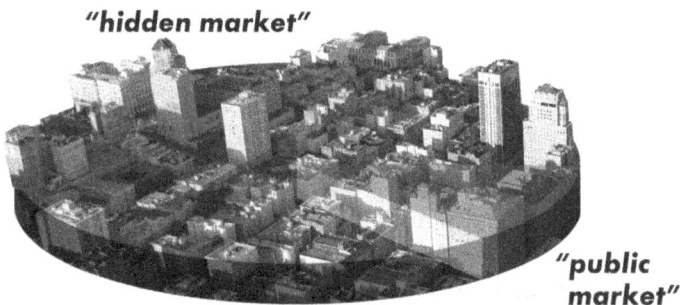

"hidden market"

"public market"

Why settle for some of the businesses for sale if you can access all of them?

Feasibility of finding a profitable business.

When we search for businesses for sale on behalf of our clients, we enable our clients to access sellers that are not otherwise available to them, to access more sellers than they can locate on their own, to find better opportunities and to locate businesses for sale by-owner where there is little (if any) competition from other business buyers. We help clients screen potential business acquisitions, whether they are for sale on the hidden market (by-owner) or represented by a business broker.

For the most part, searching for a business is a numbers game. The more people you properly inform that you are looking for a business, the better chance you will find one. The more *business owners* in your network that meet your criteria, the better your chances will be to locate specifically what you seek. To increase your chances, expand the number of business owners and people who can refer to you businesses for sale by-owner.

Few businesses will meet a buyer's criteria. Therefore, it's vital that you not taint your target list of business owners. You risk this if you don't correctly approach owners, or if you don't know how to manage your communication with sellers and their advisors. It's rare for a business, which is worth buying, to be made available by a seller to a buyer who does not make an impeccable first impression.

The *Business-For-Sale Locating & Screening System* we teach clients gives them access to the hidden market, the place where the most *profitable* businesses are for sale by-owner. It's where there is little, if any, buyer competition.

Kryptonite for business buyers weakens opportunity.

What is Kryptonite for business buyers?

Kryptonite, you may know, is the fictional substance that weakens Superman. Just a little dab will do him in.

And only two words predict what weakens or destroys the best of plans for people wanting to buy or merge companies.

Buyer competition is the Kryptonite for business buyers.

The best business brokers, for the sellers they represent, create buyer competition.

Buyers have to outbid the dumbest buyers to achieve done deals.

In case you don't know it, the best brokers provide at least 62 benefits for sellers. Go to my website and use the search box on the bottom of the webpages. Type in: "62 Reasons for Sellers Hiring Brokers."

And then read and weep if you're a buyer without a worthwhile acquisition team.

And jump for joy if you want to sell your company.

Smart buyers hire a *Business Buyer Advocate* to help level their dealmaking playing field . . . and to take buyers into the hidden market of businesses not yet for sale but can be. It's how to meet the best companies quietly for sale by-owner.

Where to find motivated sellers.

It's not like buying a home!

Some business brokers are willing to assist a buyer in their search for a business. Unfortunately for both the buyer and the broker, the market is not efficient, especially when compared to real estate. In most areas there is no Multiple Listing Service (MLS) to facilitate business broker cooperation. To further complicate things, confidentiality is a primary concern; more so than in real estate. Without a system for splitting commissions and sharing business listings, or a uniform process used between business brokerage offices, it is difficult for a broker to properly access listings outside their own office. The alternative for brokers is to provide, from scratch, custom search, analysis and dealmaking assistance on behalf of the buyer similar to what is offered by *Business Buyer Advocates*. But most business brokers are focused on the listing and selling of businesses. Full-service buyer representation is outside their core business model unless they have specific training to serve buyers.

Ask them to specifically explain their training as professional service providers to buyers and to show you their written materials (how-to info and data collection and analysis forms) they convey to buyers during their consulting engagement.

Business owners that wish to sell can be best served by using a business broker. Brokers price, package and market the business, creating buyer competition and maximizing value. Buyers should have a *Business Buyer Advocate* to look out for their best interests.

Where to find motivated sellers?

The more methods you use, the greater the probability of buying a winner. Develop and expand your network of people who know your *specific* acquisition criteria. The *typical* business buyer searches only in the public market. He simply answers for sale by-owner ads and talks to a few brokers. Too bad most owners do not sell their business that way. Stay in contact with *all* brokers, but do not limit your search to them. Go to the hidden market—it's where some of the best companies sell by-owner, where there is little, if any, buyer competition. These sellers do not advertise.

Prospect here:

- Businesses not for sale—yet

- Unadvertised by-owner sellers (hidden market)

- Personal network

- Social media

- Court records

- Broker listings (including pocket listings)

- For-sale ads

- Companies recruiting for top job

- Conglomerates spinning off divisions

- Your business-wanted ad

- Financial institutions

- Bank trust departments

- Venture capital and private equity firms

- Suppliers

- Professional advisors

- News articles

- Customers

- Competitors

- College professors

- Trade associations

- Chambers of Commerce

- Landlords

- Auctioneers

- Internet websites that advertise companies for sale

Call, write, advertise or network to find sellers?

Have you been looking for worthwhile opportunities? Not much fun, is it? Finding lots of fairly priced profitable businesses for sale? I didn't think so. And you're not alone.

It's time for Plan B. You can telephone owners. Write to them. Advertise "business wanted." Prospect for leads in networking group. Doing these things is not much fun, either. But the most successful buyers do all of these things; simultaneously. They out-source the tasks they cannot or do not want to handle. (I and my colleagues connect our clients to proven resources; finding help on the Internet is a fast way to taint your marketplace of potential sellers or merger partners.)

But, before you go directly to company owners, it is essential that you develop a list of companies that appear to match your acquisition criteria. It's a waste of time and money to call every business of the types you seek.

Telephoning?

The professionals who do this for a living know how to get past the gatekeepers; they connect with the company owner. If you love speedbumps and rejection, you can make the calls yourself.

When we show clients or their service provider how to do this, we create scripts proven to keep owners talking if they are tempted to meet a business buyer. ("Are you for sale?" rarely works.)

Writing?

Sending email hasn't worked for us or our clients. It might work for you. Or it might cause owners and their gatekeepers to blacklist your email address; you might not ever be able to communicate with them.

Mailing letters (snail mail) works, when done right. I can't share with you, in this book, a boilerplate search letter.

We customize the letters for each kind of client and target industry. We tweak the letters, too, in light of the national and regional economy.

Here is a generic search letter (which we do not use) written by Arnold Goldstein, an author of how-to-buy-a-business books: *The Complete Guide to Buying and Selling a Business*, New American Library and *How to Buy a Great Business with No Cash Down*, Wiley.

I want to acquire a retail automotive firm located within the greater (city) area, with annual cash flow (owner salary plus business net profit) in the $_____ to $_____ range. My preference is for a business specializing in used parts: however, I am flexible and will consider other opportunities.

I am a principal (not a broker) with adequate capital and financing. I can immediately purchase the right business.

If you have an interest in selling, please call me at your earliest convenience. You have my assurance that I will hold all matters in the strictest confidence. I enclose my business card for future reference in the event you have no present interest in selling. Of course, I would greatly appreciate your directing this letter to any of your colleagues within the field whose business may be on the market.

Sincerely,

Advertising?

There are numerous online and other venues to advertise your desire to buy a business. Google to see examples.

This is an excerpt from an advertisement I recently saw:

Business Wanted

I want to buy an established, profitable B2B company located in . . .

Networking?

There are numerous online venues to publicize your desire to buy a business. LinkedIn is one of them. Adapt your profile to feature what you want to achieve. Reach out to all your contacts on the various online services.

There are also industry trade associations, social and business clubs, lead exchange groups. Use them to meet company owners.

When you publicize your search / acquisition criteria, you are leading / directing people to where you want them to be instead of reacting to their boilerplate communications to you.

Here's what a client emailed me about this:

Ah yes.

I see what you mean now. You attract them. Not chase their bait. You make them chase you as best as possible. This makes perfect sense to me now.

So, the first thing you want to do is make sure that your own bait is quality. (Your resume, story, search criteria, etc.) So, we are hunting opportunities and trapping bird dogs (brokers).

Reluctance is the top reason buyers can't find winners.

Reluctance is the number one reason why so many buyers are all dressed up with no place to go: If they're not in the field or on the phone, every day, digging for referrals to sellers or talking to sellers, they might get old and die before buying a business.

People wanting to buy a business ARE selling . . . themselves . . . to people who can help them get what they want.

Ask sellers this, first.

The best way to screen sellers is not to talk to any that do not comply with your requests or do not own a company with the features you seek. If a seller's business does not comply, run don't walk away. (If a broker presents business opportunities that do not satisfy your criteria, tell him or her to only show you businesses that do.)

Referring to your acquisition criteria, select a few sample questions that enable you to quickly establish whether a business is likely to meet the rest of your specifications. If you do not get the proper response, why continue to investigate the opportunity?

For example, say something like this:

I plan to buy a business which is profitable and which is not too heavily loaded with debt. I am accustomed to earning a salary of $_____ annually; the business I buy must have a record of paying the owner at least this amount (in addition to the business' profit). Can your business satisfy these requirements?

Building a list of companies matching your criteria.

Have you discovered that business brokers rarely represent businesses for sale whose asking price exceeds $500,000? Have you also figured out that a big proportion of small businesses for sale, especially the best ones, are not represented by brokers?

If you want to buy a bigger business (or access all of the available companies), you will have to directly contact owners, nearly all of which will not be for sale nor will they want to talk about selling. That is normal. That's why we want lots of businesses to contact.

Therefore, try to expand your perspective into the kinds of businesses that could appeal to you. You can do so using bizbuysell.com and similar websites by reducing this element of your search selections: Minimum price. Drop down to $300,000, and then lower. As you drop the price, more kinds of businesses will show up in the search results.

Learn about those kinds of businesses. Try to find more than one business for sale for each kind that interests you. Compare. And determine the SIC, the NAICS and the description.

And then using DATA AXLE, INC. and other list purveyors find out how many companies are in their database.

Aim for hundreds of narrowly defined businesses (SIC / NAICS) that match your selection criteria.

The alternative for the above, and perhaps only as a test, you could decide to buy a smaller, more readily available business if you discover one during your tour of brokers and online venues. To some extent it comes down to how much time, money and effort you want to put into finding an acquisition.

Giving up is for losers.

It's not easy to find a worthwhile company to purchase or with which to merge. And it's not easy to buy the *right* business the *right* way. But you can do it if you learn from this book, and if you assemble the right team of business acquisition advisors, and if you do what it takes to achieve your goals.

Picture in your mind's eye as having already achieved this goal. See yourself doing the things you'll be doing when you've reached your goal.

— *Earl Nightingale*

Go shopping with a full toolbox of knowledge.

You are not adequately prepared to search or to evaluate and buy a business unless you have and understand all the tools and resources that a prudent business buyer uses. To list a few: Acquisition advisory team; acquisition criteria; statement of capability (resume); proof of financial capability to do a deal; general knowledge about business buying; communication scripts; data collection and analysis forms; specific knowledge about your target industries; checklist of the 22-step business acquisition steps; ability to access the hidden market of businesses for sale by-owner.

Brokers (and sellers) ask about the buyer's cash.

Brokers (and sellers) screen buyers on the basis of the buyer's cash available. Brokers, for example, do not want to waste time showing businesses for which the buyer cannot qualify or make the investment. That is good for you, too; you won't waste your time.

Confidentially disclose to brokers and sellers the highest amount of *down payment* cash you are willing to invest to purchase a worthwhile business **plus** (separately) the amount of cash you *might* invest in your company post-closing for *working capital*.

The best brokers and sellers are going to ask you to prove to them, upfront, that you have at least that amount of ready cash or cash equivalent.

Don't create conflicts-of-interest for business brokers.

Misunderstandings can arise when you interact with brokers.

Unless you hire and pay a broker to be your business acquisition advisor, with the broker pledging full loyalty to you, consider brokers to be your "bird dogs."

Think of brokers, whom sellers hire to market their company for sale, as your bird dogs. They find the birds. You shoot the birds. You don't give a bird dog your shotgun, so don't give your broker anything he could use against you.

The best brokers help you communicate directly with sellers, playing interference if communication breaks down.

Isn't finding a terrific deal a long shot?

Yes, if you make either of two mistakes:

1. Limit your shopping to where all the other buyers are shopping.

2. Don't know how to quickly put together a worthwhile deal.

It's important that you learn how to meet owners of the best companies for sale plus the companies that are about to be for sale—before they have a chance to list their business for sale with a broker. The longer brokers are on scene, the more time they have to create a *seller's* market by attracting hordes of buyers who compete with one another. (Of course, this is wonderful if you are a seller.)

Another way to access some of the best deals is to be the first buyer to see the unadvertised "pocket listings" from business brokers.

Lionel Haines, a writer and entrepreneur, says,

"You must act like a hunter, not a trapper."

You can't wait for opportunity to come around. You must seek it out, and when you find it, you must know what to do or you will lose your chance.

Know this about "off market" pocket listings.

The term, "pocket listing," appears elsewhere in this book but here let's acknowledge the value to business buyers.

This is where you can find companies secretly for sale.

Not many buyers know about the existence of pocket listings. You had to know someone who knew someone who could tell you about these opportunities. But as I write this book, I am noticing websites appearing that specialize in publicizing pocket listings with various degrees of disclosure. I'm not going to name any of them here for it remains to be seen whether these websites are a valuable addition to the dealmaking playing field. But you can easily find them online.

And there seems to be a more concerted effort by business brokers to work pocket listings. Real estate agents have been on the forefront. Business brokers are paying attention.

The definition, by investopedia.com, of "pocket listing," is any listing that is retained by a listing broker or salesperson that does not make the listing available to other brokers in the office or to other multiple listing system members.

Elaborating, *wikipedia.org*, says the reasons for a pocket listing may vary from the need for privacy or secrecy to discrimination, and some sellers may have their own reasons for not advertising a listing in conventional ways, including wanting to sell only to certain types of people. Several legitimate marketing strategies can also lead sellers to choose pocket listings. Pocket listings can be very appealing to buyers who seek exclusive opportunities. Other legitimate reasons for a seller to decide to do a pocket listing include the potential for a faster, smoother transaction when the listing agent has buyer clients who may be interested in the property. It can reduce the need for many showings to strangers.

Some company owners want to test the market for their business, to evaluate reactions by potential purchasers. It can be a good way, in a limited and controlled environment, to test various asking prices and terms of sale.

Another reason some sellers opt for a closely guarded pocket listing is if the company doesn't sell, the owner doesn't want there to be a public record, online or elsewhere, of its attempt to sell. Buyers might construe an unsuccessful effort to sell as indication of an undesirable or unsellable company.

But there is another kind of pocket listing. It's not actually a "listing" in the legal sense. It's where the agent knows an owner who wants to sell the company but it is not for sale in the usual way. It could be for sale if the agent introduces a prospective buyer to the company owner, which motivates the owner to play along with the buyer for their mutual benefit.

Another variation is the BIZFIZBO ˚ (business for sale by-owner), which is one of my registered trademarks. Here the seller may have casually brought the company to market without putting much effort into selling. Some of these wannabe sellers tell brokers: "I'll pay your sales commission if a buyer you connect me with purchases my company."

Expired listings are another source of sellers. Introducing you to sellers whose listing was not renewed is a way brokers can try to be compensated by sellers for the time and money the brokers spent trying to sell the company during the listing periods.

Professional advisors and sources of financing to companies and their owners are another source of sellers. These potential sellers are not pocket listings per se; these third parties connect buyers to potential sellers, especially when it is in their self-interest to do so. Like business brokers, these sources of referral will not waste time on unprepared or unqualified buyers.

Chuck Post, on bizben.com, writes, "It is not a myth. After a great deal of time a business broker gets to know a lot of business owners who, under the right circumstances, would like to sell their business. For myself, I am not anxious to take these listings until the seller has a true incentive to sell. If I am going to be responsible to each selling client it will require a great deal of time and continuous updates. However, sometimes that right buyer comes along that causes me to recall the business and I will contact the seller to see if he is interested. I would estimate that more than one-half of my sales come this way."

According to the blog, biggerpockets.com, pocket listing valuations tend to be more reasonable and buyers are typically bidding against fewer competitors (sometimes no competitors), who are mostly professional investors. Brad Johnson, co-founder of Park Street Partners, writing on this blog, further asserts, "I'm focusing our firm's off-market acquisition efforts on pocket listings, which I've found have a much lower bid / ask spread and a much higher 'hit ratio' of agreeing to terms and executing a purchase agreement."

Business brokers and other intermediaries disclose their pocket listings to highly qualified buyers who intend to achieve a done deal as soon as possible.

After you impress brokers with your capability to buy and manage a company, discreetly ask about their pocket listings. It can be a good thing to meet sellers whose companies have not hit the market. (On the other hand, arrogant owners with unrealistic expectations need to be knocked about by buyers in the marketplace before owners "get real.")

In most regions of the USA there is not a system similar to the real estate MLS for the marketing of businesses for sale. And most business brokers do not cooperate with each other as much as do real estate agents. Business brokers show the most qualified and well-prepared-to-buy potential purchasers their pocket listings.

— *Ted Leverette*

Various people don't want you to buy a business.

Advisors to the seller lose their job when the company sells because, usually, the buyer has his own advisors.

As you know or will find out, most of the businesses advertised for sale are (1) junk, or they are (2) overpriced or (3) a horde of buyers is competing for them. Many of the best companies, where the best deals occur, are sold by-owner to buyers who know how to properly meet and handle these sellers.

Avoid a public auction when business buying. It's a seller's market because there are more buyers than good businesses. The buyers who "win" at this auction are the ones with more cash than common sense and more greed than fear. What they usually win is a thankless job, called a "company." They are trapped, with all their personal assets on the line. These buyers struggle to survive. Many don't.

Savvy business buyers avoid competing with inexperienced buyers. They know that numerous sellers of profitable businesses don't conduct a public auction; these sellers don't want to broadcast their desire to sell, and they don't want to pay a broker's commission. The best way to find a winner business, and not compete with other buyers, is to buy direct from a seller. The problem is finding the seller.

When middlemen get squeezed.

The Motley Fool warns: "Think twice before investing in companies that act as middlemen. They're frequently price-takers on both ends, wielding little clout with their suppliers or customers. These businesses, such as oil refiners, drillers and chemical producers, can have a bumpy ride, given their weak bargaining power. They often feature low margins, high capital needs, overcapacity, and profits that swing wildly, usually at the whim of outside forces. They're not always as attractive as you might think."

Remember *The Motley Fool* warning when you evaluate middle-men such as manufacturer representatives, distributorships, whole-salers and their like.

It's not only about the company; it's about you, too.

Realize it is more about the motivation of the owner to sell than it is about the business for sale. It's a misconception to think that the most important thing you should uncover in due diligence are the business' problems and opportunities. These are important, but why bother if the seller is not serious about selling NOW? The business may be a wonderful acquisition, but you won't get it if the seller is not motivated to sell it for fair market value and upon reasonable terms.

A better deal might not be around the corner.

Don't shop 'till you drop. The longer you look for a business to buy, the less likely you'll buy one. If you upfront establish realistic acquisition criteria, it does not take long to discover winners for sale, especially if you shop on the hidden market of businesses quietly for sale by-owner. You may not want to buy the first winner, but make an offer on the next winner. There are profitable and fairly priced businesses for sale, but you may not discover them within your timetable.

More may be *less*, according to a study that says shoppers are 10 times more likely to buy if there are 6 choices than if there are 24. Barry Schwartz, *The Paradox of Choice*, writes: "The old argument is that the more choices you add, the more you improve the collective welfare. This turns out not to be true." Too many choices can lead to paralysis (by analysis) and dissatisfaction. Too many choices cause us to waste time making decisions and worrying that we might be making mistakes. Buyer confusion can be followed by buyer remorse if the buyer imagines that a better deal was available elsewhere.

The worst case we saw was a former CEO who wasted two years to find 205 sellers (in various industries) of which 40 were excellent acquisitions. He kept postponing his decision to buy because he thought there would be a better deal down the road. The business he bought was no better than most of the winners that he saw early in his search.

Getting ahead of yourself is a good way to trip.

Once you've established your acquisition criteria and advisory team, and before you call on business brokers and sellers, visit banks and other sources of financing. Tell them about the types and sizes of businesses you want to buy. Ask each potential source of financing to what degree they might have interest in furnishing acquisition or post-acquisition financing. During the process of surveying lenders and investors you will garner tips about business buying and you will collect intelligence about the industries that interest you. If you can't line up sufficient financing (which is conditioned upon you presenting a good deal that complies with their lending/investing standards), you will know that it is mandatory to buy a business from a seller who will finance you.

The best way to interact with people is not to draw them or be drawn into conversations about due diligence and evaluating companies. Simply let people know, if they try to involve you before you are ready, that at this time you are simply screening opportunities. (This book provides you with tools for screening.)

Proceed with a realistic, tentative acquisition timeline.

We developed a *Street-Smart 22-Step Acquisition Sequence*™ to help our clients avoid pitfalls and stay on track.

You can derive your own steps and benchmarks within these major categories: preparation, search, due diligence (legal, financial, HR, operational inspections, risk management, marketplace, etc.), financing (current and potential), valuation (assets and enterprise), dealmaking (negotiations, contracts, escrow, closing, etc.) and post-purchase due diligence and transition management.

Control the time clock and the sequence of events.

Searching for the right deal can take much longer than you expect. Getting the deal done, the right way, can be more time consuming than you think. Your anxiety will be less if you have an experienced business acquisition team. They can tell you what is normal, in real time as you go along. Too many dumb deals transpire because of buyer impatience.

Remember when your influence is most powerful.

You probably have the most influence over the seller between the date of the letter of intent and/or the purchase contract and the date scheduled to close the transaction. If you have properly crafted your letter of intent and definitive purchase agreement and other documents pertinent to your pending transaction, and if things occur that reduce the business' potential, you can have legitimate reasons to change the terms of purchase. Of course, if you made the mistake of trying to buy a business that is attracting other buyers, the seller may tell you to take a hike.

Qualify the seller; determine worthiness /opportunity.

Without being intrusive, you can politely test the seller's motivation to sell. Ask these questions: Do you own the real estate that houses the business or do you lease the premises? Why are you selling your business? What are you going to do after you sell your business? What price do you have in mind? Do you have a valuation from a business appraiser as the basis for your asking price? Are you willing to provide any financing to your buyer? By when do you want to complete the sale? Do you have interest in a working partner, someone who buys part of your business now and the rest later? Who else has an ownership stake in your business? Are they as committed as you are about selling? Who is the attorney that will represent you in the sale?

If the "seller" won't answer these questions or if he provides weasel answers, you may be wasting your time. You may not want to dump this seller, but you would be wise to aggressively search for more deals.

Hand the owner a *Seller's Disclosure Statement*. The one we use causes the seller to take a stand on some of the most crucial issues, some of which can be major impediments to the sale.

Is it for sale or is the seller testing its marketability?

Just because a business is offered for sale does not mean it is really for sale. The owner may be testing the market or looking for free business advice from eager business buyers. "I'm burned out" is not a good enough reason to sell, unless you're meeting the owner in a mental health unit or the cardiac care section of a hospital. If the seller does not have a compelling reason to sell, you should have other deals in your hopper. Don't waste time on a non-motivated seller, but go to school on him to learn about the business and its industry. He won't be as open with you after you purchase one of his competitors.

Does the owner have a compelling reason to sell?

The owner must have a compelling reason to sell, or it is highly likely you will overpay and make unnecessary financing and other concessions.

Owner's catastrophe signals your buying opportunity.

These are some of the catastrophes adversely affecting the business *owner*, and not necessarily adversely affecting the company, which give owners a compelling reason to sell:

- Divorce

- Death

- Disability

- Burnout

- Retirement

- Family feud

- Partnership dispute

- Bank calls the owner's personal loan

- Owner can earn a better return elsewhere

- Company is part of a larger firm that wants out of this line of business

- Company outgrows owner

- Owner is an entrepreneur and wants to create not manage

These situations give you the opportunity to buy the right business the right way.

Company's catastrophe can be your buying opportunity.

These are some of the catastrophes adversely affecting *companies*, which give their owners a compelling reason to sell.

- Owner dies without succession plan

- Catastrophic natural event

- Uninsured damage or legal claims

- Unprecedented loss of sales

- Governmental actions or seizures

- Political decisions

- Sudden financial write-down or write-off

- Fraud or theft

- Wrong business decision

- Court judgment against the business

- Restraining legal action

- Strike or labor disruption

- Expiration of financing

- Lender changes terms of financing

- Involuntary bankruptcy possible.

These situations, if you know how to cope with them, give you the opportunity to buy the company on terms favorable to you.

First two questions to ask sellers.

It's a good idea to begin by asking sellers to explain why their company is for sale.

And then ask sellers to justify their asking price.

These questions generally get the *least* reliable answers. That's why the rest of your questions must slip behind the seller's rhetoric and defenses, so you can ferret out the truth.

The asking price should not scare you away.

As they say in real estate, you can pick the price if I can choose the terms of purchase. Don't let the asking price kill the deal. I am not suggesting you overpay for a business unless there are good reasons to do so, which you confirm with your acquisition team in the context of your financial and strategic plan.

Fish with a net, not a line.

Too many buyers set themselves up for defeat because of their poor positioning during search. Typical buyers do not cast a wide enough search net. So, they decrease their odds of buying a company, and it takes longer to achieve a done deal, because they have so few choices.

Don't unnecessarily narrow your search.

A *Business Buyer Advocate* will help you identify numerous types of businesses that fit your financial and managerial capability so you can sooner buy a worthwhile business.

Don't limit your search to readily available sellers.

Act like a hunter, not a trapper. You cannot wait for opportunities. Efficiently seek them. When you find one, know exactly what to do in the 22-step business acquisition sequence. Do not settle for a loser if you cannot find a winner. The obstacle is your method of searching for businesses for sale, not a lack of good companies.

Don't be wedded to a particular type of business.

Just because a particular type of business appeals to you does not mean you should forego looking at others. Don't marry a commitment to a single industry. Business buying is a journey of exploration.

Include the possibility of a partial ownership stake.

If you think the only way to buy a business is buy an entire business upfront, think again. There's an alternative that can be safer and more profitable for you and the seller. Purchase a working "partnership" in the firm. Buying a stake in the right business can put you in charge and it can position you to buy the remainder later. Owners who are not ready to retire and/or are burned out may be open to this because it is a way to diversify their risk and convert into cash (or other assets) some of the net worth tied up in their business.

Consider winner businesses in lousy industries.

Sometimes fabulous opportunities arise to purchase longstanding profitable businesses, which have sustainable competitive advantages, in troubled industries. In fact, the winner businesses can become stronger as the weaklings fail or are forced to sell for pennies on the dollar. Of course, it would not have been a good idea to own the last surviving buggy whip manufacturer. So, do your homework to assess the industry.

Lemmings join the crowd at their own peril.

Corporate downsizing creates a horde of unemployed, inexperienced business buyers, many of whom are desperate to buy themselves a job. They congregate around sellers who advertise to attract buyers and broker-listed businesses because these are the easiest ones to find. Few of these people know how to buy a company. They're a major threat to you because they naively bid up the price and the down payment. They create a seller's market! Don't join the crowd of business buyers.

Bidding during the seller's auction can cost you.

If you want a particular business and the only way to get it is to outbid competing buyers, have the discipline to not bid more than the business is worth; resist accepting terms of purchase that are not good for you.

Don't let big dog competing buyers beat you.

Can you show the seller your advantages, such as your direct experience that fits what the company needs or how your way of doing business will be more acceptable to the customers, employees or suppliers, or that you can make faster decisions about closing the pending transaction and the closing will not be as complicated as it may be if the owner tries to sell to a big dog?

Don't shop/buy via Internet; window-shopping is okay.

Don't use your mouse to buy a business. Window-shop online the thousands of businesses for sale that are listed on numerous websites. These websites are a good place to see what's available to the general public and to glean details about various industries.

But beware: If you can find these sites, so can other business buyers. That means buyer competition, most of which is ignorant competition, which means the least knowledgeable buyer wins the competition to buy.

Shop beyond business brokers—way beyond.

There is nothing wrong with beginning your search for an acquisition by calling all the brokers in your area. You might be able buy a mature, profitable and fairly priced business listed for sale by a broker. But don't stop with brokers.

Advertising puffery can snooker you.

Advertising puffery can cause a business buyer's dream to become a nightmare. Instead of reading the funnies this Sunday, read the online advertisements (they're entertaining!) of companies for sale. Screenwriters are creative. So are advertising copywriters. But the award for encouraging language—with the goal to exchange your money for someone else's business—should go to business sellers.

Beware of online commentary and social messaging.

Don't neglect to monitor online commentary and social messaging. Search for references to the company for sale, its owner(s), its key employees and the other "*C.E.L.B.S.* ™ (i.e., customers, landlord, bank and suppliers).

Be aware that what you read could be bogus chatter, paid reviews, whether positive or negative.

You've seen "flaming," haven't you? It is defined by urbandictionary.com: "An online argument that becomes nasty or derisive, where insulting a party to the discussion takes precedence over the objective merits of one side or another."

Don't be deceptive with sellers.

You take a huge risk if the seller discovers you have misrepresented your sincerity or capability to buy his business. You might be liable for the time, money, lost opportunity and damages to the business that the seller can attribute to you posing as a legitimate business buyer.

Don't do something stupid in a seller's market.

A seller's market exists whenever more than one buyer is vying for the business. Access the hidden market of businesses quietly for sale by-owner; they represent as much as 80% of the sellers of the most profitable companies for sale, depending upon the industry.

This topic is controversial. My opinion comes from my experience working for buyers.

I want to share with you something sent to me by a credible business broker. I won't identify him because of the controversy surrounding this topic, but you need to widen your vision. In any market there are good and bad businesses for sale. There are businesses that are hot, and not, at any given time, which means more buyers compete for them. In those cases, buyers must move quickly, but still follow the advice in this book. Going through a long-drawn-out due diligence process before entering into an earnest money contract or letter of intent to purchase causes buyers to lose what could be a good business. (Too many buyers, proceeding without the right acquisition advisory team, make due diligence and dealmaking more difficult and time-consuming.)

The broker goes on to say, "In my experience, about 30% of the businesses that change hands do so between the seller and seller's family members or to an existing employee. These businesses are never 'On the Market.' Only about 30% of the businesses change hands outside of family members, close friends, or employees without the use of a broker. That means about 40% of the businesses that change hands today are done by brokers."

Don't be too quick to reject sellers.

Sellers know more about their business than they tell you early in your due diligence. This includes vulnerabilities and opportunities. If the business is profitable, continue your research into it until the facts show that the vulnerabilities negate the opportunity.

Are your values consistent with the industry's values?

I'm referring here to morality and how you view right and wrong. Some industries play looser than others when it comes to doing the right thing all the time. If that is not your style, you will not be comfortable or effective in those industries. Likewise, at the company level, the internal culture may be lacking the degree of ethical conduct you prefer, or the cultural behavior may be more rigid than you like. Trying to change company culture is about as likely as successfully turning your spouse or children into what you want them to be. And changing an entire industry? That is for Don Quixote.

Biting off more than you can chew can choke you.

It's no fun to have a wildcat by the tail. It is usually not wise to purchase a business that will immediately require a capability larger than what you bring to the table. Don't buy a business that is too big or whose growth will consume resources faster than you can provide them. Shy away from a firm whose technology is alien to you. If you are not intimately familiar with the line of business, it can get away from you shortly after you buy it. It's not a simple task to absorb knowledge from the seller and the business' employees during your transition into a business that is strange to you. If you're a Type B personality, a volatile business not may be best for you.

Don't be overcome by technology.

Is technology changing faster than the company?

Newspapers are being diminished or replaced by online sources. Hewlett-Packard was deleted from the Dow Jones Industrial Index because it did not keep up with or remain on the cutting edge of technology, and the company is struggling with finding its way. Radio Shack stores are being killed by online competition. Apple, at the time of this writing, has outrun Microsoft despite Bill Gates' 1998 proclamation in a *Vanity Fair* interview that he "couldn't imagine a situation in which Apple would ever be bigger and more profitable than Microsoft." Google is scaring investors because some of its numerous forays into disruptive innovation are not paying off.

Changing technology, if you cannot keep up with it, can adversely affect your business too. Effective engagement with social media, automation, computers and software can disrupt your workforce, which means you simultaneously have two problems: Integration of technology and nervous employees and customers (and maybe suppliers). Marketing and other communications are increasingly becoming affected by electronic media. Retailing and financial services are being hit hard by changing technology, especially by the Internet. So, during due diligence and after closing, do what it takes to anticipate change and decide how the company will adapt to it. What resources, such as capital investment and training, will be necessary?

Investigate governmental influences.

You can quickly discover important facts and vulnerabilities about companies if you check the courts and the various governmental agencies that regulate the businesses.

Consider this example: Many cities host green markets where local vendors (mostly micro businesses) sell fresh fruit, veggies, meat, fish, bakery products and handmade goods. They are popular with nearby residents and a fun way to while away a weekend morning. However, in many locales the merchants complain about governmental ordinances being confusing, inconsistent and unfair. It is becoming increasingly costly for merchants to participate. Numerous green markets across the nation have folded their tents.

Evaluate and seek info from trade associations.

Not checking with the industry's trade association is like buying a dog without looking into the characteristics of the breed.

Don't be lazy.

Search non-stop, with intensity, for a business to buy until the day you buy a business. If you don't have the discipline, time or energy to do this, hire someone to do it for you. The excellent opportunity that you fail to uncover is the deal you should have done.

Paying attention pays.

Don't be so focused on tracking your target business that something jumps out to bite you. Don't be so preoccupied with the hunt that you miss important clues. Pay attention to the marketplace, which means where you live and the location of the business and its customers. Read the daily newspaper, the local business press and trade journals. Stay in touch with business brokers. Ask your *Business Buyer Advocate* to uncover businesses for sale by-owner and to tell you what s/he learns when s/he is making inquiries on your behalf. Keep a log of what brokers and sellers say is the typical ranges of asking prices and profits for businesses like the ones you want to buy. Visit every seller of a business if it is the type you seek; don't ignore it because of its problems, location or price. You might only have one meeting, but what you learn could be invaluable.

Manage disputes; don't unnecessarily fear them.

You will disagree with and be offended by sellers, brokers, advisors and family. That is the way it is with business buying. Getting angry and losing a deal is self-destructive. Look for common ground; go to it; invite the other side to join you and then negotiate from where you agree. Whenever you want to lash out at someone to put them in their place, think about reggae music. Many reggae tunes have a lilting rhythm and feel-good melody, yet the lyrics harshly state what's wrong in the world. Because it sounds good the bad news goes down easier.

Don't be insulting.

Too many wannabe buyers insult sellers and their representatives; this can end the possibility of a worthwhile done deal. The most attractive sellers dump buyers who are impolite, excessively demanding or don't efficiently handle due diligence and the buying process. These behaviors motivate some sellers to "bad-mouth" the buyer among the seller's friendly competitors. Similarly, brokers might warn their friendly competitors about nuisance buyers.

Don't denigrate business brokers.

The broker you insult today could be the broker who introduces you to buyers when you're ready to sell your business. Don't be critical of the quantity or quality of broker listings. Their job is to market businesses listed for sale. Brokers do not represent all the sellers. It is your job to find the rest.

How brokers flame bad buyers.

(Recommendation to buyers: Behave yourself!) It's normal for people in business to trade marketplace intelligence. Sometimes they warn their peers, even their competitors, about bad actors. Here's an excerpt on LinkedIn, posted by a business broker in a group catering to brokers:

My firm has been contacted on two separate listings by _____.
Beware. At minimum he lacks the sophistication to be a viable buyer.

Too many buyers ignore these red flags.

Some of this deserves repeating because too many buyers in the heat of business buying forget the importance of critical situations, especially when they are *screening* potential acquisitions. Use this as a checklist to remind you of actions you can take to improve your business, or the company you buy or start. These are the kinds of situations, if too many exist within a potential acquisition, that cause savvy buyers to move on to another opportunity; they don't want to waste their time and money for in-depth due diligence. Alternatively, if you are looking for a troubled company, which you think you can turnaround into a winner, this checklist provides ideas you can deploy.

According to *Forbes*, "Steel Versus Silicon:"

- "Of the 100 largest U.S. companies in 1917, only 15 of them survive today. The other 85 went bankrupt, were liquidated, were acquired or were left behind. A mistake, unless very quickly corrected, could be fatal. A small edge, expertly exploited, could rocket a small outfit way ahead of its competitors. Take nothing for granted. Examine every premise."

Some businesses suffer a profit hemorrhage because they are plagued by many of the items on our list. Others are doing so well that they are not aware that profit is leaking because of inattention to a few areas.

Incoherent business plan.

The plan is a guide to profit only if it is logically consistent and if it is a working document. Review it in its entirety before making any decision that differs from what the plan anticipates.

Minor changes in one area can have an impact on other parts of your business.

Most problems are traceable to an owner who does not recognize how decisions impact the business beyond the obvious areas.

Your financial plan deserves two parts: where you will probably be in the next few years and where you want to be. Begin by learning the true market value of your business (the price a buyer would pay today). If this amount is less than you estimate or the value is not sufficient to fund your retirement, seek outside counsel on profit and value maximization strategy.

Working capital misunderstood.

A precise accounting definition aside, working capital means the surplus cash to finance your business when cash expenditures exceed cash receipts.

Most businesses do not know when or how much working capital is necessary. You cannot accurately answer the question until you identify monthly cash flow for the past two years and forecast it for the next three years. Not knowing when a cash crunch will occur is a major cause of bankruptcy. It is also why an owner sells a distressed business for pennies on the dollar to an investor who has enough cash to relieve the cash crisis.

Build a cash cushion.

Customer satisfaction underrated.

It is not enough to satisfy customers; they must be delighted. They must tell their friends how wonderful you are.

If you do not already have elated customers, you probably will not get them until a consultant properly diagnoses what is wrong and educates you on how to make improvements.

Failure to use creative financing.

People in business and people who want to own a business share a common problem — MONEY. Specifically, not enough money at the moment they need it.

Your lack of capital is a hindrance you can overcome with street-smart knowledge of finance.

Take these three steps to get the capital (debt and/or equity) you need when you need it:

1. Properly prepare yourself and your company—to attract money. Mistakes will cost you more than hiring a consultant.

2. Know all the techniques savvy people use—and how to choose applicable ones.

3. Know sources of funds—and the best way to approach them.

Do this now; do not wait until you are under financial pressure.

Confusing spending with investing.

A dollar spent is a dollar lost unless it produces more than a dollar of income. Do not spend money unless you know how the expenditure will increase sales or reduce costs.

It is naive to believe you are getting a valuable tax write-off when you spend money. Spend a dollar, and at most you save fifty cents in taxes, but in fact you are still fifty cents poorer than had you not spent the money.

Control your overhead. It is easy to incur expenses that seem reasonable in themselves, yet cumulatively add up to more than you can afford.

Blue eyes—red feet.

Many owners love to gaze at blue sky—what ought to happen or how much better things will be.

Meanwhile, they are oblivious to the red ink gathering around their feet. Reversing a downward slide is very difficult.

Being a know-it-all.

AKA owner-centric. There is not enough time for you to do everything in your business, let alone to know how to do it all.

Successful operators appropriately delegate responsibilities to expert employees and advisors.

Self-confidence can disable your business if it stops you from getting timely and useful professional advice.

Too many businesses suffer from the all-controlling owner who not only knows how to do everything but also insists on being part of everything.

One of our colleagues, John Martinka, author of *If They Can Sell Pet Rocks Why Can't You Sell Your Business (For What You Want)?*, writes: "When the owner makes him or herself the most important cog in the operations, it's called a dependency; buyers, bankers and appraisers watch out for this. Don't let yourself be the bottleneck. Business buyers may pass or offer a lower amount when they see how big the shoes they have to fill are."

Paying for quantity instead of quality.

This problem surfaces when you hire low wage people with average abilities instead of adequately paying highly competent ones. It also occurs when you do not make a sufficient investment in things that are visible to the public, such as fixtures, shopping bags, brochures, letterhead, signs and your online presence.

If you cannot substantiate that your business can afford what it requires to succeed, your business may not be worth starting or owning.

Inappropriate advertising or publicity.

Do not spend for advertising without setting measurable goals for a sales increase as a direct result of the ad.

Don't trust online advertising venues click/impression reports.

Sales rarely increase immediately; they rise at an expanding rate in relation to an effective and continuing advertising program.

Your plan must track the response and compare it to the goal.

Discontinue a program that is not achieving interim goals.

Advertising costs money; publicity may not. Get the public's attention!

People must instantly think of your business when they need what you sell. Otherwise, they might visit your competitor.

A pro in getting publicity should continuously schedule stories in the media about your business or you.

Newsletters to customers get people talking about you.

Unusual sales/promotions create traffic and get media coverage.

Not asking for a price reduction or better payment terms.

Recently we told the tenants of a shopping center to get quotations on insurance from competitors to their carrier. Only one person made the attempt. She made two phone calls and immediately saved $600.

Landlords may reduce rent before your lease expires. Ask.

Not knowing when to shut down.

Going out of business is not as bad as it can get. It is worse to take a long time to fail, all the while losing money.

Monthly accurately assess whether your business is worth more than it was last month. If it is not or if you are in doubt, do a shutdown analysis.

Do not throw good money after bad. Optimism is fine, but don't jeopardize your personal financial security by unwisely transferring your savings into your company.

Consider getting an opinion from us. We specialize in helping owners improve or sell their business.

Resting on your laurels.

People are intolerant of businesses whose service declines. It does not take much to shift a customer's loyalty to your competitor. Getting it back is not easy.

Product design is not fixed in stone. Identify the "must have" features of your products. Continuously improve their performance.

Your customers will perceive you as the market leader and innovator.

Your benefits include an increase in your profit and market share, plus better customer satisfaction.

If you do not improve, expect your competitors to do so with their products, at your expense.

Being ill-prepared to transfer success.

Many businesses fail because the owner got into a field for which he was ill-prepared.

A smashing success in another business, or as an employee, is not always transferable when people start or buy a company.

Lack of persistence.

It takes longer for some types of businesses to make a profit. Do not give up until you are certain you have tried everything to make it work.

A business plan helps because it enables you to test decisions without the risk you assume when you test a decision in actual operations.

Reacting to your business.

This is putting-out fires. Substitute management for reaction, to make it easier to operate your business.

Your written business plan identifies potential problems and records their solution. When a problem occurs, simply implement the solution that is in your plan.

Improper insurance.

It is important to know your risk, and obtain insurance to cover it. If you are sued, with proper insurance, your carrier handles and pays some or the entire claim. Otherwise, your business becomes weak when you are absent from it to defend yourself and pay legal fees and settlements.

Ignoring your family.

Trouble at home frequently leads to business problems. It is easier to pilot your business when the rest of your life is in order.

Isn't your responsibility to build financial security for your family? Your business can contribute three ways: Maximization of profit; provision of a succession plan to handle your exit; taking advantage of tax loopholes.

Wrong location.

Each type of business demands a certain kind of location. If you do not properly locate your business, you will work harder and assume more risk. Moreover, careful study of locations appropriate to your type of business can save you rent because less expensive premises may be sufficient.

Improper inventory.

For retailers, this means knowing how to balance supply and demand and how to prune inventory to eliminate obsolete or slow-moving merchandise.

Service businesses sell time; therefore, time management is vital.

Sell products/services for which there is proven demand. Even the largest corporations have trouble changing consumer preference.

The wrong price.

This applies to what your business sells, and when you sell your business.

Price too high, repels buyers; too low, invites skepticism.

Price sensitivity can sometimes be overcome by offering creative credit terms.

The marketplace is not the only determinant of price. What you charge relates to your cost of doing business and the buyer's perception of value.

Price must meet your profit target while you are in business, and fund your retirement when you sell out.

Most owners work hard for years under the mistaken belief that their company is worth more than it actually is.

Now is the time to know the maximum price a buyer will pay.

The sooner you find out, the more time to improve your company.

Break-even point?

Knowing how to compute the break-even point for every decision you make which affects income or expense saves you from many mistakes.

Management by committee.

Refer to others for opinions before you make decisions, but minimize the decisions you make by consensus.

Doing it for practice.

Business is not where you try ideas with the intent to make corrections as you go along.

The first time out of the box is frequently the only opportunity you get.

Planning enables you to do it right the first time.

Being blind to the competition.

Assume competitors are wolves in sheep skin. They may be tame when you are doing well, but at the first sign of your distress, they can kill you.

How often do you evaluate your company's competitive advantages?

Competitive advantage exists when a company's profit and reputation is above the norm for its industry. It occurs when the company is more capable than its competitors at managing the resources available to it, such as a superior product with outstanding value proposition.

Failure to recognize key trends.

Stay aware of changes in your industry, among your competition and your customers.

Example: It was common knowledge a couple of years before each Boeing downturn that production of airplanes would drastically decline, causing Boeing to lay off tens of thousands of employees. This adversely affected suppliers to Boeing, the vendors to the Boeing suppliers, and businesses that serve Boeing employees.

Wise owners took steps to protect themselves before the problems arose.

When your customers' needs change, seize the opportunity to supply the solution to their problem.

If your customers do not notice improvements you make, you may lose customers to your competitor.

Diversification without synergy.

Do your homework before you add products or services, or enter a new market segment.

Diversification can expand your products/services and increase your profit—if you have adequate financial and managerial resources to support growth.

Without synergy between your existing product line and/or customer base and what diversification creates, you can dilute your resources and hurt your business.

Inadequate checkup.

The Business Vitality Checkup ™ we do for our clients plugs profit leaks, eases tension and unlocks the value in their business.

The most important, and last, question buyers fail to ask.

Too many buyers don't ask sellers and their representatives this question:

"Is there any information that you know of that you have not disclosed to me, which might have a bearing on the viability or the value of the business for sale?"

Worse, too many buyers asking the question let the seller get away with a non-definitive answer.

Here's a tip: Get the seller's answer to this catch-all question in writing and make it part of your purchase and sale agreement.

Chapter 7

How to BUY the Right Business the Right Way

You've been reading *How to **Prepare** Yourself and **Find** the **Right** Business to **Buy***.

If you're not sure you know everything you need to know so you can safely and profitably proceed from identifying what appears to be one or more potential acquisitions, read my other book, *How to Buy the Right Business the Right Way*, which you can access from my website: PartnerOnCall.com.

Due Diligence & Evaluating Companies

Thorough pre-acquisition due diligence of the company's value and risk increases the probability that you will buy the right business the right way. With each potential acquisition, begin by establishing your primary point of contact, which is someone who knows enough about the business to accompany you throughout your evaluation of the company. This person should help you gather relevant documents and help you schedule interviews of people within and outside the company.

This chapter shows how to do it, so you can avoid pitfalls along the way.

Pricing / Valuing the Company

"Accurately valuing a small business is often the most challenging part of the process for prospective business buyers. However, it doesn't have to be an overwhelming or difficult undertaking. Above all, you should realize that valuation is an art, not a science. As a buyer, always keep in mind that the "Asking Price" is NOT the purchase price. Quite often it does not even remotely represent what the business is truly worth," writes Richard Parker, president of The Business For Sale Buyer Resource Center™.

This chapter shows how to do it, so you can avoid pitfalls along the way.

Financing Your Acquisition and the Company

The Great Recession and its aftermath, including the credit crunch, has resulted in an increase in seller financing, creative financing, asset-based lending and alternative sources of capital for buyers. This chapter details what is happening and what to do about it.

Negotiating and Dealmaking

How you design and handle negotiating and dealmaking determines your success.

This chapter details what is happening and what to do about it.

Closing the Sale / Purchase

Escrow and closing the sale / purchase of a company is a critical time in dealmaking. It can be complicated. It is when pending transactions can falter.

This chapter details what is happening and what to do about it.

When You're in Charge

It is a critical time when you first walk into the company you bought, especially during the first ninety days. You will be overloaded with work. Customers, employees, suppliers and other people and organizations will be anxiously watching you. It's when you discover whether or not you bought the right business the right way.

This chapter details what is happening and what to do about it.

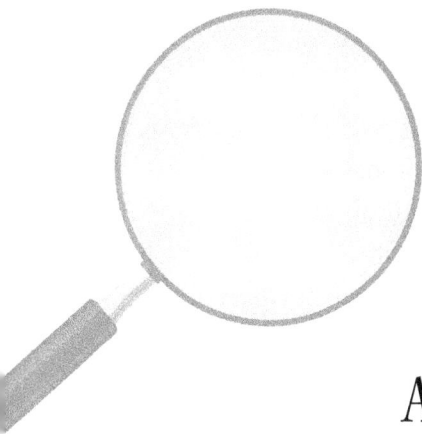

Afterword

Here's how this book came into being and how it evolved over the decades.

Let's start with my admission. I was snookered when I bought the *right* business the *wrong* way—proving the saying: Success does not always breed success.

I've guided hundreds of buyers as they acquired mature, profitable, fairly-priced companies having sustainable competitive advantages. I've purchased or invested in twenty-nine small or midsize businesses. Twenty-eight were winners. But early in my career I took a bath on one of them. So, how I did I get snookered? My dream became a nightmare because, before I bought it, I did not do a good enough job investigating the seller and the company.

Had I adequately deployed the due diligence process, which I use with my clients (some of it summarized in this book), I might have detected the risks before I closed on my misguided transaction. My legal team got me out of the mess thanks to my well-drafted purchase and sale agreement. I lost money, sure, but it could have been much worse.

I pledged, from then on, to devote most of my business life to helping people avoid mistakes so they could profit from business ownership. Since my disastrous acquisition, I've been noting mistakes people make during their business buying activity, some of which I observed while consulting with clients; other errors were reported to me by the independent professional advisors trained in the use of my trade secrets, know-how and dealmaking tools.

What you read in this book comprises less than 10% of what is in the materials available to our *Business Buyer Advocates*˚. Their materials and client reference guides show how to handle various tasks, using our proprietary methodologies and our data gathering and analysis forms.

Contact me for help: PartnerOnCall.com.

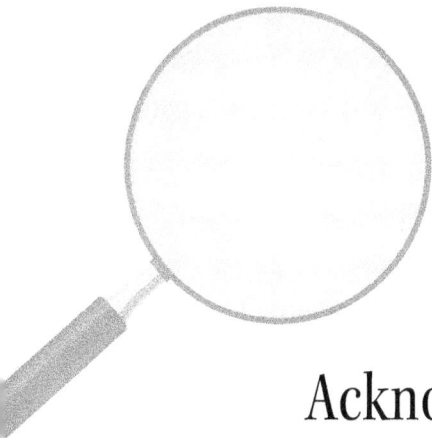

Acknowledgements

How to Prepare Yourself and Find the Right Business to Buy
How to Buy the Right Business the Right Way

The *Dos, Don'ts & Profit Strategies,* in those books, and my success, would not be as large if not for these people. I don't know everything about buying the *right* business the *right* way, but I know enough dealmakers with state-of-the art expertise to whom I can turn when I need facts, tips and strategies.

Thank you, first, to my tolerant and supportive wife, **Kathy**, who has put up with me since the 1970s, during my three retirements, and with me becoming bored and going back to work despite her telling me to play more and work less.

John Martinka, MBA, known as "The Escape Artist," since 1993 has been a valuable contributor to my success. He helped establish "Partner" On-Call Network, LLC, taking time away (five years!) from his successful consulting practice to train and collaborate with people we trained to use our system of consulting. His e-newsletter, *Getting the Deal Done,* is in my inbox. His two books are on my desktop: *Buying a Business That Makes You Rich* and *If They Can Sell Pet Rocks Why Can't You Sell Your Business (For What You Want)?*

Robert Nice, a highly successful financial analyst, company manager, real estate investor and consultant, all before beginning to use our system of consulting in 1995, inspires me whenever he empowers people to buy the right business the right way, or helps clients improve and then later profitably exit their companies.

A few more, in alphabetic order:

- **Alan Fox**, who used our dealmaking tools and know-how to acquire a mid-market size company, the revenue of which he quadrupled. And then sold for a BIG profit. He became a *Business Buyer Advocate* in 1998. For several years he outperformed all of us with respect to income and diversity of transactions. He has helped clients buy, start, improve, finance, value and sell small and midsize businesses.

- **Steven Beal**, MBA, CGA, CFA, CBV, CBI, in 2005 was the first Canadian we trained to use our consulting materials. He went on to diversify his business buyer advisory and business improvement consulting practice to include business brokerage. His example encouraged me to train business brokers and other professionals.

- **Bob Biggerstaff**, "Serial Entrepreneur," founded and managed several companies one of which was recognized by *INC. Magazine 500*, and earned the *Ernst and Young Entrepreneur of the Year Award*. In 2008, after briefly trying but becoming bored with retirement, we trained him. By 2013 his consulting firm had grown and diversified beyond the scope of work most of us perform. While not presently a member of our network his influence on us continues to benefit us.

- **David Barnett**, a Canadian we trained to use of our consulting materials, helped "Canadianize" for Canadian readers my creative financing book, *How to Get ALL the Money You Want For Your Business Without Stealing It* ™, which until the "translation" did not include topics that are Canadian-specific.

- **David Sweeten**, CBI, CPA, BCB, LREB, owner of a business brokerage, was the first brokerage we authorized to use our business consulting materials. Ideas he shares enable me to relate better to the "other side" of the dealmaking table, business brokers, from my buyer-side view of transactions.

- **Fayaz Karim**, BSc, MBA, CPA, Chartered Accountant (Canada), residing / working in the USA, since 2002 has provided me with useful and truthful insight into what really happens within franchise systems. He uses our consulting materials to diversify his longstanding franchise development and consulting activities to include *Business Buyer Advocacy*.

- **Howard Katz** took our training in 1995. It didn't take long for him to do two things that materially increased his success and my success. Within a few months using our consulting methodologies he expanded and monetized one of our client services, which before then I viewed as a minor byproduct of our consulting. His success motivated our *Business Buyer Advocates* to emulate his methods, which substantially increased their income and better-served their clients. He was the first among us to use our consulting know-how to purchase a company for his own account. From that point onward, I have encouraged people in our business to consult AND buy and sell companies for their own account.

- **John Gallagher**, CPA, owned a thriving accounting and tax practice. In 1995 he decided to diversify deeper into business buyer advisory, using our proprietary tools. And then he showed us the power of our know-how when he, over several years, between consulting engagements, bought and sold numerous companies for his own account.

- **Loren Marc Schmerler**, a Certified Professional Consultant and Accredited Professional Consultant, helps business owners understand and maximize their bottom line. His newsletter has given me ideas I have put to successful use.

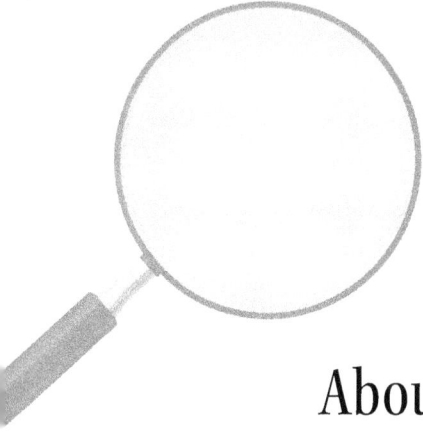

About the Author

Business Buyer Advocacy ™ and the *Hidden* Marketplace

The goal of *"Partner" On-Call Network* ° (and the people we train to become advisors to business buyers) is to facilitate the safe, profitable transfer of businesses, as quickly as possible—so every party to the transaction gets a win-win deal.

In the 1970s, Ted Leverette figured out how to access the "hidden" market of the best small and midsize businesses quietly for sale by-owner. This is important because most business buyers access only about 20% of the mature and profitable companies for sale, the ones represented by brokers or advertised to the general public. When those buyers find sellers on the "public" market, they are among a horde of buyers who congregate around those sellers. These buyers can cause a bidding war among themselves, which means businesses can sell for more than they are worth (which is a good thing if you want to *sell* your business).

Of course, Leverette had to have a name for his discovery of the way to introduce buyers to the best businesses for sale, of which up to 80% are on the *hidden* market. And then guide buyers through evaluation and dealmaking, with loyalty only to the buyer. So, he coined and trademarked an advisory title: *Business Buyer Advocate* °.

The idea worked well for many years, so Leverette decided to teach other people how to consult with business buyers. These consultants use his trade secrets, know-how and dealmaking tools in their independently owned and operated consulting practices in the USA and Canada.

Their 500-year collective experience gives their clients more leverage than is otherwise possible.

"Partner" On-Call Network LLC is not a business brokerage; we don't list businesses for sale and then take them to market; independent users of our information might be. We collaborate with and recommend the best brokers. Brokers reciprocate by referring clients.

Diversifying or Becoming an Advisor to Business Buyers

The Street-Smart Way to Become a Business Consultant™ is what you get from us if we share with you the use of our trade secrets, dealmaking tools and know-how. You can be credible because our niche is unique, valuable and fun.

Day one our testimonials can become yours. You benefit from our network of leading attorneys, accountants, appraisers, brokers, sources of financing and other specialists who help us achieve done deals. Plus, you gain access to the most profitable companies in nearly every industry, some of which are quietly for sale by-owner on the hidden market; these winners you can introduce to business buyers.

Please contact me from my website (PartnerOnCall.com) if you or someone you know might want to use of our trade secrets, know-how and dealmaking tools to consult with business buyers . . . or be introduced to a *Business Buyer Advocate*.

About Our Founder — Ted J. Leverette

Mr. Leverette, The Original *Business Buyer Advocate*˚, since 1974 has advised business buyers and owners on buy/sell, valuation and business improvement.

Since 1993 he has taught advisors in the USA and Canada to use our methodologies: *The Street-Smart Way to Become a Business Consultant* ™. They independently own and operate their consulting practices. Nearly 3,000 people connect with him on LinkedIn. He earned the *Small Business Hero Award* "for outstanding small business achievement and assistance to the community" from the Service Corps of Retired Executives Association (SCORE). He has been a lecturer for colleges, trade associations. He's the author of podcasts, articles and books.

Media appearances include *1490 WGCH, Financial Survival Network, Wall Street Journal, USA Today, The New York Times, The Palm Beach Post, The Seattle Times, Washington CEO Magazine, Eastside Business Journal, San Jose Mercury News, Entrepreneur Magazine, The Business Insider, Small Business Opportunities, Centre For Small Business Financing, Small Business Opportunities, StartupNation, The Certified Business Counselor, American Venture Magazine, richardparker.com, bluemaumau.org, bizbuysell.com, bizquest.com, Business Brokerage Press, DiscoverU.*

How did Ted Leverette get started in this business?

"In the 1970s, while doing various kinds of business consulting, I began to help corporate executives who wanted to quit their job and buy a business. Quickly I discovered that some of the best businesses for sale were not advertised or listed by business brokers or other kinds of intermediaries. When I contacted owners of companies quietly for sale by-owner, and told them a business buyer had paid me to help find a good business to buy, these sellers were delighted, especially when I also told them that they would not have to pay me, and that I was not functioning as a business broker (i.e., wanting to list their business for sale and earn a commission) but instead was working on behalf of and paid by buyers as their *Business Buyer Advocate*.

"I have trained people who want to use my trade secrets, know-how and dealmaking tools in their independently owned and operated consulting practices. Some of these people did not want to do much consulting; they wanted to use the consulting platform to buy and sell businesses for their own account, consulting with business buyers between their personal dealmaking activities."

What he can do for you.

"My guidance enables people buying small and midsize businesses to achieve more profitable done deals sooner with less aggravation and at lower cost. How? Read my how-to books. And then let me help you deploy my proven best practices.

"I can help you assemble and quarterback your advisory team on the basis of my experience seeing too many dysfunctional teams."

"You can absolutely, positively count on me to do my best to help you achieve the success you seek."

— *Ted J. Leverette*

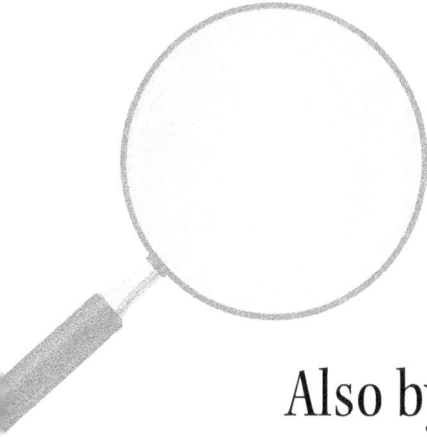

Also by Ted Leverette

How to Buy the Right Business the Right Way ™

How to Get ALL the Money You Want For Your Business Without Stealing It ™

21st Century Entrepreneur Ideas for Kids and Aspirational Adults ™

120 Financial Lifelines for Small Businesses ™

Food & Fun on the Central Coast ™

The Best of the Central Coast ™

Some of these books are available only to the clients and users of the "Partner" On-Call Network LLC proprietary system of consulting:

- The Street-Smart Way to Become a Business Consultant™
- Business Buyer Training Syllabus™
- Business-For-Sale Locating & Screening System™
- Business Acquisition System™
- Business Profit Maximizer™
- Business Seller Training Syllabus™
- Preparing a Business for Sale™
- The Street-Smart System to Start a Business™
- *Franchise Evaluation and Selection System* ™

Appendix

Bill of Rights

Bill of Rights for Buyers of Small & Midsize Businesses ™

(Reprinted with permission from the publisher.)

Creation and development of this Bill of Rights.

This first edition of the *Bill of Rights for Buyers of Small and Midsize Businesses* ™ exists because people envision a more harmonious, safe and profitable playing field for business buyers, sellers and their service providers.

In 2011 we began the creation of this *Bill of Rights* by requesting ideas from business buyers and from every kind of service provider with whom buyers and sellers interact. People suggesting ideas for the *Bill of Rights* are mostly from the USA and Canada. A few contributions are from Europe, South America, Africa, Asia and Australia.

Preamble

We buyers want the truth, the whole truth and nothing but the truth *before* less than full disclosure has the opportunity to adversely affect us.

Fundamental Rights

Protection
from dishonest people.

Access
to *all* the businesses for sale, and to useful service providers.

Service
from competent, legitimate business brokers, M&A intermediaries, business acquisition advisory specialists, and other professional service providers.

Information
that is timely and that accurately discloses details about businesses for sale, and about everyone with whom buyers interact during their process to evaluate and purchase a business.

The Bill of Rights for Buyers of Small & Midsize Businesses

1st.   The right to expect a worthwhile, accurate, credible explanation about the content of the business acquisition process from service providers.

2nd.   The right to an oral or written agreement with business acquisition advisors and/or business brokers and intermediaries to represent the buyer's self-interest; not favor the seller during the buyer's process to purchase a business.

3rd.   The right to be treated by business acquisition advisors in a way that demonstrates their attempt to protect the buyer from unfair or unintended consequences.

4th.   The right to be exposed to all relevant acquisition targets regardless of said target's representation or lack thereof by another service provider or the sellers and/or sellers' service provider's willingness to split fees or provide other financial consideration to buyers' service provider.

5th.   The right to know the rules governing "Transaction Brokers," which permit such brokers to list for sale a business and work with a buyer interested in it if the agent complies with the law of agency (i.e., authorized to act on behalf of a principal to create a legal relationship with a third party, the effect of which may include limited confidentiality for the buyer and seller and more focus on facilitating a done deal).

6th.   The right to be informed about the seller's reason(s) for sale.

7th.   The right to be informed about the seller's perception of the business' competitive advantage(s), which position it to sustain or improve its competitive position.

8th.   The right to be informed of the seller's opinion about the condition of the economy in each geographic region in which the business serves a material quantity of customers, and about the effect of the economy on the company.

9th.   The right to be informed of the seller's candid opinion about the business' weaknesses, including factors that currently or probably will inhibit it from achieving its potential.

10th.   The right to be informed about the seller's estimate for the annual capital expenditures necessary to operate the business at its present amount of gross revenue.

11th.   The right to be informed about the degree to which the business relies upon owner or one or more key employees, the loss or replacement of which is likely to adversely affect the business' profitability or viability.

12th.   The right to be informed of "sweetheart" transactions or relationships existing or existed between the business and any party, especially transactions that under- or over-state the business' revenue or expense or gives it any advantage.

13th.   The right to be informed about business revenue (i.e., skimming, barter, etc.) and expense (i.e., barter or not paid with the business' money) of the business not reported on the company's financial statements and tax returns.

14th.   The right to be informed about the business' off-the-books revenues or expenses (i.e., cash sales, employee accrued but unpaid time off, pension contribution, etc.)

15th.   The right to be informed if the business uses vehicles, equipment or other assets that it does not own, lease or rent.

16th.   The right to be informed about the degree to which the business' revenue is sensitive to seasonal or cyclical factors.

17th.   The right to obtain from sellers and/or their representatives accurate, timely information if the business is in default on financial, non-financial, warranty, taxation, contractual or other obligations, and pending or unpaid claims (not disclosed on the business' financial statements) for back wages, rent, supplies or anything else, and about easements, zoning and surrounding property uses, availability of utilities and who provides them, certificates of completion re: construction and build-outs, environmental, natural or geological hazards affecting the real property or the business.

18th.   The right to be informed of the business' contingent liabilities, including but not limited to pending or actual disputes with employees, customers, etc.

19th.   The right to investigate whether the business or any of its owners are the subject of a bankruptcy filing, assignment for benefit of creditors or insolvency proceeding of any kind.

20th.   The right to be informed about customers that account for more than 5% of annual gross revenue or if the loss of any customer is likely to materially adversely affect the viability of the business for sale.

21st.   The right to be informed of commitments to employees, independent contractors, service providers, suppliers or sources of financing regarding an increase of their compensation.

22nd.   The right to be informed of the identity and job description employees or independent contractors related to the owner of the business or one another.

23rd.   The right to be informed about actual or probable disputes with the landlord or problems with the business' premises.

24th.   The right to be informed about substances, materials or products on or near the premises which may be an environmental hazard such as, but not limited to, asbestos, formaldehyde, radon gas, paint, solvents, fuel, medical waste, surface or underground storage tanks, contaminated soil or water.

25th.   The right to be informed about the remaining useful life of the business' fixtures, equipment, vehicles, intangible assets, etc.

26th.   The right to be informed if the business is subject to a franchise, distributor or licensing or other restrictive agreement.

27th.   The right to be informed whether the business or any of its owners or employees is required to have any license or permit, and to confirm compliance thereof.

28th.   The right to obtain from sellers and/or their representatives accurate, timely information about pending zoning changes, redevelopment or nearby construction that may affect the business and about covenants, conditions and restrictions in connection to contractual or governmental issues that the business is or will be subject to.

29th.   The right to be informed of alleged violations filed or under investigation by authorities issuing licenses or permits or with respect to the violation of laws or regulations.

30th.   The right to be informed of unresolved insurance claims.

31st.   The right to an honest and prompt response to this question: Is there any information known to you that has not been disclosed to me in writing which might have a bearing on the viability or the value of the business for sale, or adversely affect the operation of the business, or a buyer's decision to purchase it, or the price a buyer might pay for it?

32nd.   The right to expect business brokers and M&A intermediaries hired and paid by sellers to inform buyers upon request about the pros and cons of businesses for sale presented by the agent, unless the agent or the agent's firm is the listing agent, in which case the agent will disclose information in accordance with legal requirements.

33rd.   The right to have access to professional assistance for the purpose of inspecting or evaluating businesses for sale with respect to operational issues and compliance with governmental rules or regulations, the intent being to know the degree to which the characteristics of the business might affect the life or the value of the business.

34th.   The right to share confidential information with profession-al advisors, service providers and sources of financing that routinely advise or serve business buyers during their process to purchase a business.

35th.   The right to request and obtain credible and reasonably up-to-date information about businesses for sale and businesses that have sold, which are materially similar to the businesses for sale the buyer targets as a potential acquisition.

36th.   The right to reasonable and timely access to and adequate response from the people and organizations with whom buyers in-teract during the course of purchasing a business.

37th.   The right to request and obtain professional guidance or as-sistance to determine the need for and availability of insurance (or other means of mitigation) to protect the potential business acquisi-tion against various usual and customary risks that may arise after closing.

38th.   The right to request and obtain from service providers refer-rals to professionals and resources that the buyer deems necessary to evaluate businesses for sale or purchase them.

39th.   The right to expect honest, full disclosure (within the con-straints imposed on agents by their fiduciary agreement with sellers) from sellers and their business brokers and intermediaries.

40th.   The right to personally inspect the assets of the business prior to purchase, including during due diligence and to verify no change in the condition of assets prior to closing.

41st.   The right to require buyer's agents or business acquisition advisors not to divulge sensitive and confidential information about the buyer to business sellers, their agents and representatives nor anyone else, without the buyer's prior written consent, and not to use or disclose buyer's sensitive and confidential information before it is time to do so.

42nd.　The right to expect service providers that serve buyers to be informed about the trends and marketplace affecting business opportunities.

43rd.　The right to receive upfront, from pending sources of financing, written full disclosure of all the conditions, fees and costs associated with the financing.

44th.　The right to competent professional assistance in the preparation of and submission of funding applications to sources of financing, the intent of which is to obtain the best terms reasonably available given the condition of the potential business acquisition and the marketplace in which the business and the sources of financing operate.

45th.　The right and opportunity to choose sources of financing for the buyer's purchase, which may differ from the businesses existing economic relationships.

46th.　The right to commit sources of financing to the terms of their financing proposal between the time of the commitment and the closing of the buy/sell transaction (i.e., last minute change of financing terms can upset the pending deal)

47th.　The right to a valuation (at buyer's expense) of businesses for sale that reflects and explains in layman's terms the most probable pricing range within which the business will sell, taking into account facts known by the appraiser about the seller's and the buyer's reasons or motivations to consummate a buy/sell transaction; and to facilitate the valuation process, to obtain from sellers and/or their representatives accurate, timely information to properly establish a market value or purchase price.

48th.   The right to expect business valuators to perform with non-advocacy, and to be assured by valuators to whom the buyer is referred that the valuator's opinion of value will not be influenced by the potential of more referrals from the source of referral whether or not the valuation opinion is consistent with the wishes of the source of referral.

49th.   The right to precede a contractual offer to purchase with a nonbinding letter of intent, which specifies major topics, which could be "deal breakers."

50th.   The right to expect business brokers and intermediaries who represent the seller not to disclose the buyer's purchase offer to another potential buyer of the target business for sale.

51st.   The right to expect service providers to avoid conflict-of-interest by not engaging in dual agency without disclosure to the parties of a transaction.

52nd.   The right not to be forced to use any particular kind of legal document except (and subject to review by the buyer's legal counsel) non-competition, non-disclosure / confidentiality and seller's agent disclosure forms prepared by the seller or seller's agent.

53rd.   The right to expect agents, service providers and salespeople not do anything that causes the buyer to become obligated to any ancillary service provider, including sources of financing, before having a fully executed contract to purchase, without the buyer's advance written permission.

54th.   The right to have competent professional legal assistance whose aim is to facilitate a done deal when reviewing contracts, and timely guidance and presentation of materials before the closing of the transaction.

55th.   The right to be the control party of the letter of intent and/or the definitive purchase agreement, with the buyer having the responsibility to pay for the production of these documents.

56th.   The right to request and obtain professional guidance or assistance during negotiations that occurs between the buyer and the various people and organizations that interact with the buyer during the course of purchasing a business.

57th.   The right not to be required to submit an offer (binding or non-binding) until adequate opportunity to review personally and with advisors relevant financial and other data regarding the company and its operations.

58th.   The right not to be required to submit a deposit, earnest money or other consideration until adequate opportunity to review personally and with advisors relevant financial and other data regarding the company and its operations.

59th.   The right to propose a stock purchase transaction in lieu of an asset purchase transaction. This can cause a change or disengagement of intermediaries and advisors due to state and federal laws pertaining to the sale of securities versus business opportunities.

60th.   The right to negotiate the structure of the transaction as buyers see fit, including the purchase price, terms of down payment, buyer promissory note to seller, transition assistance, date of closing and notification of stakeholders, such as customers, employees, landlord, sources of financing and suppliers.

61st.   The right to disengage from dealmaking with sellers when sufficient reasons arise to abort the potential acquisition.

62nd.   The right to expect legal counsel to explain how the buyer can get out of a business before getting into it (i.e., tactics and contractual escape clauses).

63rd.   The rights for buyers (and others) to unilaterally cancel agreements on the basis of mutually agreeable escape clauses, with (if any) cancellation penalties or liquidated damages clearly spelled out in the agreement.

64th.   The right to purchase contract contingencies on the buyer's deferred payments to the seller, including the parameters of earnout provision.

65th.   The right of offset in the purchase contract, which means the seller is obligated to refund some or all of the purchase price to the buyer or reduce or eliminate deferred payments due from the buyer if the seller's warranties, representations or other contractual commitments turn out not to be true.

66th.   The right to purchase contract provisions pertaining to seller warranties and representations, including the consequences (such as a right of offset) if the seller misrepresents or violates warranties and representations.

67th.   The right to request that the seller cease marketing the business for sale ("no shop" provision) in return for buyer depositing earnest money into escrow, which may or may not be refundable depending upon the terms of their agreement.

68th.   The right to negotiate purchase contract restrictions on the seller's conduct before the closing of the buy/sell transaction.

69th.   The right to obtain reasonably early in dealmaking the necessary third-party actions or consents, so assure a done deal and avoid delays during the closing of the transaction.

70th.   The right to renegotiate or terminate the proposed transaction without penalty if the buyer detects (and can show evidence of) the seller's material misrepresentation or insufficient disclosure about the business.

71st.   The right to abort the pending transaction without penalty, or to obligate the seller to modify the purchase price or terms of sale or make repairs at seller's expense if damages arise or deterioration (beyond normal wear and tear) occurs to the business between the time the definitive purchase and sale agreement is executed and before closing of the buy/sell transaction.

72nd. The right to commit the business' landlord to the terms of the lease assignment proposed by the landlord between the time of the commitment and the closing of the buy/sell transaction (during which the assignment becomes binding upon the agreed terms).

73rd. The right to collaborate with the seller during dealmaking to negotiate retention terms with the business' key employees so they remain with the business for a reasonable amount of time after closing of the buy/sell transaction.

74th. The right to prompt and accurate notifications from or concerning sources of financing, landlords, key employees, key customers or suppliers that differ from what was promised or represented at the time the buyer and seller mutually reached their agreement.

75th. The right to expect business acquisition advisors in the employ of the buyer, and within the scope of the assignment, to reasonably educate the buyer and provide knowledge useful to the buyer's evaluation and purchase of a business for sale.

76th. The right to be informed before the event occurs about the conditions, relationships or communications that commit the buyer to work exclusively with an agent, business broker or intermediary that represents businesses for sale or provides business acquisition advisory services.

77th. The right to expect business acquisition advisors to suggest alternative negotiating strategies and tactics with sellers and others with which the buyer interacts during the course of purchasing a business.

78th. The right upon request from the buyer for the buyer's service provider(s) to accompany the buyer during one or more of the buyer's visit to businesses for sale and meetings with the seller or the seller's representatives, or attending and providing assistance to the buyer during closing of the buy/sell transaction.

79th. The right to expect service providers such as attorneys, business brokers and intermediaries who represent the buyer or seller to promptly present all legal written offers buyers want conveyed to sellers.

80th. The right to expect service providers not to unnecessarily or unfairly disrupt dealmaking and deals.

81st. The right to expect business acquisition advisors to think and act independently, which best serves the buyer's self-interest.

82nd. The right to a reasonably long survival period after closing of the seller's warranties and representations (i.e., there should be recourse against sellers if written warranties and representations, memorialized in the purchase contract, turn out not to be true).

83rd. The right to expect service providers to honor their fiduciary relationships whether pledged or established by behavior.

84th. The right to contractual (in addition to legal) recourse against sellers that misrepresent information about themselves and their businesses for sale.

85th. The right to reasonably request and obtain a continuing relationship between the selling owner and the business after the sale of the business, which when properly presented by buyers can be acceptable to sellers especially if the seller provides financing for the buyer's purchase.

86th. The right to advice or assistance after closing by professional service providers with expertise in post-sale management transition and due diligence.

87th. The right to expect service providers, with or without the buyer's request, to refer buyers to other knowledgeable service providers whose reputation is a dealmaker instead of an unnecessary deal killer.

88th. The right to request that business acquisition advisors, business brokers and intermediaries not have a pending or potential investment in the business for sale and simultaneously be a consultant or business valuator to the business buyer or seller.

89th. The right to request from people purporting expertise in business valuation or pricing businesses for sale to show supporting evidence of adequate qualifications.

90th. The right to expect service providers to refrain from providing service on the basis of race, religion, gender or national origin.

91st. The right to expect sources of referral not to recommend or employ unqualified business appraisers or where conflict-of-interest may exist.

92nd. The right to expect service providers to suggest specialty talent which can benefit the particular buyer's situation.

93rd. The right to expect service providers not to accept remuneration from other than the buyer with respect to the buyer's intended acquisition without the buyer's written permission to do so.

94th. The right to expect service providers not to seek or take benefit from inside information that may become known to them during the course of serving buyers without the buyer's advance written permission.

95th. The right to expect service providers to promptly inform buyers of special relationships, circumstances or interests that might influence or appear to influence the service provider's counsel, objectivity, judgment or recommendation concerning the buyer's intent to purchase a particular business.

96th. The right to expect service providers to comply with and encourage buyers, sellers and others with which buyers and sellers interact to comply with laws, regulations and sound business practices in the conduct of the business.

97th. The right to be advised of any related party transactions affecting the business.

98th. The right to be informed if any employees are on work release or of any other status that may affect workplace safety.

You made it to here, so you've probably expanded your perception of what you can accomplish. May I suggest that you order my creative financing book?

How to Get All the Money You Want
For Your Business Without Stealing It ™.

It's another tool for success.
— Ted Leverette

List of Topics

www.ingramcontent.com/pod-product-compliance
Lightning Source LLC
Chambersburg PA
CBHW060335200326
41519CB00011BA/1943

* 9 7 8 1 7 3 7 0 1 1 9 0 3 *